D0214886

ORTHODOXY

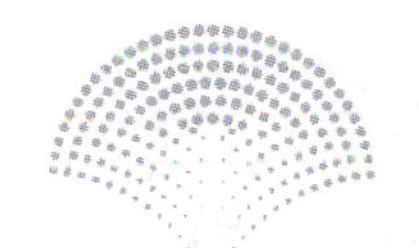

ORTHODOXY

G. K. Chesterton

With Annotations & Guided Reading
by TREVIN WAX

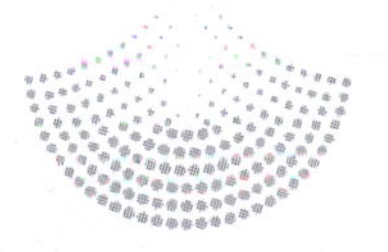

ACADEMIC
NASHVILLE, TENNESSEE

Orthodoxy: With Annotations and Guided Reading by Trevin Wax

Published by B&H Academic
Nashville, Tennessee

ISBN: 978-1-5359-9567-2

DEWEY: 239
SUBHD: CHRISTIANITY / THEOLOGY,
DOCTRINAL / APOLOGETICS

Cover design by Ligia Teodosiu.
Cover pattern by Kloroform/Creative Market.

Printed in the United States of America

1 2 3 4 5 6 7 8 9 10 VP 27 26 25 24 23 22

Dedication

To my mother

CONTENTS

INTRODUCTION TO G. K. CHESTERTON AND *ORTHODOXY*

Where should we start when considering Gilbert Keith Chesterton? I struggle to describe him, beyond the general description of "writer." What kind of writer was he? He wrote poetry, perhaps best represented in *The Ballad of the White Horse* and *Lepanto*. But he was much more than a poet. He also wrote works of philosophy, apologetics, and history—often debating with the luminaries of his time, whether in person or on the page.

Should we begin with his art and literary criticism, of which his *Charles Dickens* is considered a classic, that introduced him to larger audiences? Or maybe his travelogues that contained his observations of different cultures? Some would point to the novels he wrote; the mind-bending *The Man Who Was Thursday* stands out. Chesterton's friend and intellectual opponent George Bernard Shaw thought highest of Chesterton's plays and always wished he would lean more into his identity as a playwright. But Chesterton was too busy as editor of a newsweekly, while dictating books on economics, culture, and society. Above all, he wrote essays—thousands of them over a period of nearly four decades, appearing in newspaper columns worldwide. First and foremost, Chesterton saw himself as a journalist. Interestingly, a century later, he is best known not for his essays but his detective stories, most notably *Father Brown*.

Not knowing how best to describe Chesterton's prolific output, I turn to an accidental work of the great writer, a work never intended for publication: *Platitudes Undone*. This rare book is a facsimile edition of *Platitudes in the Making* published in 1911 by Holbrook Jackson, a disciple of Nietzsche and Fabian socialism. Jackson communicated his progressive "wisdom" through a collection of short and memorable statements, properly categorized for the readers of his day. In celebration of the book's release, he sent a copy to Chesterton, who, with a green pencil, proceeded to work his way through Jackson's book, commenting on nearly every one of the platitudes.

A few of my favorites:

- **As soon as an idea is accepted, it is time to reject it.** *No: it is time to build another idea on it. You are always rejecting if you build nothing.*
- **Truth is one's own conception of things.** *The Big Blunder. All thought is an attempt to discover if one's own conception is true or not.*
- **No opinion matters finally: except your own.** *Said the man who thought he was a rabbit.*
- **Don't think—do!** *Do think! Do!*
- **Every custom was once an eccentricity; every idea was once an absurdity.** *No, no, no. Some ideas were always absurdities. This is one of them.*
- **Doubt is the prerogative of the intellect; Faith, of the emotions. Nowadays the emotions have all the Doubt and the intellect all the Faith.** *The mind exists not to doubt but to decide.*
- **The great revolution of the future will be Nature's revolt against man.** *I hope Man will not hesitate to shoot.*
- **Love is protective only when it is free.** *Love is never free.*

Chesterton tested the platitudes of his age with countercultural thought and humor. Slogans and sayings, new terms and shifts in language, ideas that gain a foothold and then spread throughout our society—he believed all of them should be put to the test of deliberative evaluation. In *Orthodoxy*, Chesterton's most famous work of apologetics (*The Everlasting Man* is probably his best apologetic book), we see this countercultural thought on display, with writing that sparkles with wit and wisdom and wonder.

G. K. Chesterton's Impact

Gilbert Keith Chesterton was born in England. He lived from 1874 to 1936. In the 1890s, while a student at the Slade School of Art, he experienced a period of profound pessimism and despair, due in part to the philosophical currents swirling about during that time. In his autobiography he describes himself "plunging deeper and deeper as in a blind spiritual suicide" before he revolted: "I hung on to the remains of religion by one thin thread of thanks." Groping his way toward a mental equilibrium based on a foundational first principle—that existence is better than nonexistence—Chesterton emerged from this experience and began to write. He began his career in 1900 and married Frances Blogg a year later. He wrote more than fifteen million words in his lifetime.

Chesterton's impact was and still is significant. In C. S. Lewis's autobiography, *Surprised by Joy*, Lewis commented on his first encounter with Chesterton's writing: "In reading Chesterton . . . I did not know what I was letting myself in for. A young man who wishes to remain a sound Atheist cannot be too careful of his reading." Chesterton's work became part of Lewis's journey to faith. "I had never heard of him and had no idea of what he stood for," Lewis wrote, "nor can I quite understand why he made such an immediate conquest of me. It might have been expected that my pessimism, my atheism, and my hatred of sentiment would have made him to me the least congenial of all authors. . . . Liking an author may be as involuntary and improbable as falling in love." Lewis, the author famous for *Mere Christianity* and *The Chronicles of Narnia*, considered Chesterton's *The Everlasting Man* to be "the very best popular defense of the full Christian position I know."

Chesterton's influence was significant among other key figures of the twentieth century. Mahatma Gandhi translated one of Chesterton's essays in the *Illustrated London News*, an essay he described as leaving him "thunderstruck," which later influenced his book *Hind Swaraj*, a key source for inspiring the movement to end British rule in India.

Of Chesterton, T. S. Eliot wrote: "If I were to state his essential quality, I would say that it is a sort of triumphant common sense—a joyous acclaim toward the splendor and the powers of the soul."[1]

Marshall McLuhan, the respected Canadian philosopher and commentator on media theory and the influence of technology, wrote: "He is original in the only possible sense, because he considers everything in relation to its origin."[2]

Scott Randall Paine claims that the uniqueness of Chesterton lies in "precisely his fusion of the philosophical with the rhetorical, the imaginative and even the charitable. Perhaps the fullness of these harmonized endowments could best be captured by saying that he possessed an Augustinian imagination, a Thomistic intellect, and a Franciscan heart."[3]

We could multiply the tributes to Chesterton issued from his contemporaries and from leaders today. I submit just one more, from H. L. Mencken, a man who stood opposed to Christianity yet acknowledged *Orthodoxy* was "the best argument for Christianity I

---

[1] T. S. Eliot, "Obituary Note," *Tablet*, June 20, 1936, 785.

[2] Marshall McLuhan, "G. K. Chesterton: A Practical Mystic," *Chesterton Review* 10, no. 1 (February 1984): 83; and McLuhan's introduction to Hugh Kenner's *Paradox in Chesterton* (New York: Sheed and Ward, 1947), xii, xix.

[3] Scott Randall Paine, *The Universe and Mr. Chesterton* (Brooklyn: Angelico Press, 2019), 14.

have ever read—and I have gone through, I suppose, fully a hundred."[4] It is to *Orthodoxy* that we now turn.

Brief Background on *Orthodoxy*

Dale Ahlquist, president of the Society of Gilbert Keith Chesterton, says, "If you only read one book by Chesterton—well then shame on you—but if you only read one book by Chesterton, it has to be *Orthodoxy*. (However, if you read only *Orthodoxy*, you had better read it more than once.)"[5] I agree. This is the best entry point into Chesterton's work, especially if you are most interested in Chesterton's role as an apologist for the Christian faith.

How did *Orthodoxy* come about? Chesterton's parents were nominally religious, baptizing Chesterton as an Anglican although they held to Unitarian beliefs. Once Chesterton emerged from a period of pessimism in the late 1890s, his philosophy of life became increasingly visible in his writing. In the early 1900s, he took part in a long-running debate over religion with Robert Blatchford of the *Clarion*. The debate focused primarily on theism against determinism; he did not delve into the particulars of the Christian creed.

In 1905, *Heretics* was released—a book that featured Chesterton's interaction with many of the leading thinkers of his day. In chapter after chapter, Chesterton argued with his contemporaries, combining the sharpness of intellect and stylistic verve that readers had come to appreciate in him. *Heretics* caused a stir, but to Chesterton's dismay many leading thinkers treated it superficially, as if his dazzling wit and rhetorical skill were merely a game for entertainment purposes. In 1937 Émile Cammaerts wrote of Chesterton's opponents:

[4] H. L. Mencken, quoted in S. T. Joshi, *God's Defenders: What They Believe and Why They Are Wrong* (Amherst, NY: Prometheus, 2003), 86.

[5] Dale Ahlquist, *G. K. Chesterton: The Apostle of Common Sense* (San Francisco: Ignatius, 2003), 22.

> They talked of his brilliant "fireworks" and of his "delightful paradoxes" when he was delivering his soul to them. They treated him as a conjurer when he spoke with the earnestness of a prophet, when his juggling was as sacred to him as a prayer, as the juggling of the juggler of *Notre-Dame*. They said that he dazzled them when he tried to open their eyes, and that he deafened them when he tried to open their ears. They confused the act and its motive, the words and the intention which dictated them.[6]

One of the reviewers of *Heretics* issued a challenge: the writer claimed he would consider his own philosophy of life only if Chesterton was willing to disclose his. Chesterton had critiqued contemporary philosophies, but he had not yet done the work of revealing his own. *Orthodoxy* was the book that came as a result. Chesterton was just thirty-four.

First published in 1908, *Orthodoxy* has never been out of print. "It is a dated work, dealing in the categories and concerns of Chesterton's contemporaries," acknowledges Matthew Lee Anderson, "and yet it comes nearer to timelessness than anything we have today. Though *Orthodoxy* was written near the start of the 20th century, I have dubbed it the most important book for the 21st."[7]

How to Read *Orthodoxy*

Orthodoxy is not a typical work of apologetics. It is the chronicle of an intellectual journey. In it, Chesterton describes a quest to found a new religion, a philosophy of life that will include everything that makes most sense of the world. Once he arrives at the end of his journey, he realizes the religion and its philosophy already exist. It is Christianity.

---

[6] Emile Cammaerts, *The Laughing Prophet: The Seven Virtues and G. K. Chesterton* (n.p.: ACS Books, 1937), 17.

[7] Matthew Lee Anderson, foreword to G. K. Chesterton's *Orthodoxy* (Chicago: Moody, n.d.).

Orthodoxy is not an easy book. One reason it can be difficult at times is because of the historical and temporal distance between Chesterton and us. Unlike his initial readers, we are not familiar with many of the people and places he mentions. But the biggest reason that *Orthodoxy* can be a challenge is that you are reading "one of the deepest thinkers who ever existed," according to Étienne Gilson, the renowned Thomist scholar.[8] *Orthodoxy* is a workout for the mind. You will walk away feeling worn out as well as invigorated. If at first you feel more of the former than the latter, you're not alone.

The good news is there's no reason *Orthodoxy* has to be harder to read than it should be. I've done what I can to lessen the more challenging aspects of this book. For example, in line with the custom of the day, Chesterton wrote in lengthy paragraphs, sometimes spanning one or two pages. In order to enhance readability, I have inserted paragraph breaks and headings, so that the flow of Chesterton's argument becomes easier to discern. (I realize that inserting paragraph breaks and headings requires a judgment call in interpretation, but I trust that longtime readers of *Orthodoxy* who might disagree with some of my choices will still appreciate my efforts to make Chesterton more accessible to contemporary readers.) I have also updated the spelling in a number of instances.

Throughout the text, I've added annotations that give more detail on the people, events, and scriptural references Chesterton mentions. I sought to be more comprehensive than sparing in order to make the book more accessible to readers of all levels and backgrounds. My goal is to get you reading Chesterton without feeling so overwhelmed by his general knowledge and expertise that you give up. (That said, once I've left a note explaining who a certain person is, I do not leave another note about the same person if Chesterton mentions him or her again later in the text. You're on your own!)

[8] Étienne Gilson, quoted in Maisie Ward, *Gilbert Keith Chesterton* (New York: Sheed and Ward, 1942), 620.

As a sidenote, if you were to read articles or books on just the people Chesterton mentions in this book, you'd get a crash course in England's history as well as the leading philosophies just before and after the turn of the twentieth century. In this way, reading Chesterton is like entering a new world, or, better said, it's entering *our* world with a trustworthy guide whose knowledge covers the terrain of history, philosophy, and theology.

I've been brief in my comments to each chapter on because I do not want to delay your getting into Chesterton's work by adding my own. My comments are designed to help you understand the lay of the land, so you can discern the pathways of Chesterton's brilliant mind and be able to follow the argument. I leave a few "memorable parts to look for" at the outset as well, so that you'll keep your eyes open for the areas of *Orthodoxy* that are most notable.

At the end of each chapter, my summaries intend to do just that—summarize what Chesterton has said, in order to make it easier to move forward to the next chapter and not forget what has gone before. Like any exercise routine or mountain-climbing endeavor, you're better off enlisting a partner or two than trying on your own. For this reason, I've included discussion questions at the end of each chapter to facilitate good conversation around the central aspects of Chesterton's work.

Orthodoxy feels at times like a cross between looking for golden nuggets in a dense jungle and whirling around on a roller coaster. Enjoy the ride. Keep the treasure.

PREFACE

This book is meant to be a companion to *Heretics*,[1] and to put the positive side in addition to the negative. Many critics complained of the book called *Heretics* because it merely criticised current philosophies without offering any alternative philosophy. This book is an attempt to answer the challenge. It is unavoidably affirmative and therefore unavoidably autobiographical. The writer has been driven back upon somewhat the same difficulty as that which beset Newman in writing his *Apologia*;[2] he has been forced to be egotistical only in order to be sincere. While everything else may be different, the motive in both cases is the same.

It is the purpose of the writer to attempt an explanation, not of whether the Christian Faith can be believed, but of how he personally has come to believe it. The book is therefore arranged upon the positive principle of a riddle and its answer. It deals first with

---

[1] Chesterton's book *Heretics*, published in 1905, was a collection of twenty essays interacting with the leading thinkers of his day and explaining why he believed so many of their most popular ideas to be wrong.

[2] John Henry Newman's *Apologia Pro Vita Sua* (Latin for "A Defence of One's Own Life") was published in 1864 as an answer to Charles Kingsley of the Church of England. Newman quit his position as the Anglican vicar of St. Mary's, Oxford, and became one of the nineteenth century's most famous and influential converts to the Roman Catholic Church.

all the writer's own solitary and sincere speculations and then with all the startling style in which they were all suddenly satisfied by the Christian Theology. The writer regards it as amounting to a convincing creed. But if it is not that it is at least a repeated and surprising coincidence.

Gilbert K. Chesterton

ONE

The first chapter of *Orthodoxy* is the shortest (and easiest to read). Chesterton sets out by introducing the purpose of this book and by giving us one of his most famous parables: the tale of the yachtsman. Fans of the late singer/songwriter Rich Mullins might recognize in the song "Creed" a few lines inspired by Chesterton's introduction. The lyricist wrote of his conviction that it was what he believed that made him who he was. He didn't make himself, the song says; his beliefs were making him. It was the Word of God—"the very truth of God"—and not any human invention. In other words, the lyrics seem to say, it was no man-made philosophy that shaped the songwriter, but God's own Word, which the singer had embraced and which was continually shaping his character.[†]

Chesterton's goal in this chapter is to explain his approach and rationale for the book, and also to introduce humanity's "double spiritual need" to be happy in the world but not completely comfortable in it—to be astonished at this world and yet feel welcome here. In seeking to solve the riddle of why we have this double need, Chesterton set out to discover and propound a new philosophy, only to find it was Christian orthodoxy.

[†] Rich Mullins and Beaker, "Creed," in Mullins, *A Liturgy, a Legacy, & a Ragamuffin Band*, Reunion, 1993, studio album.

Memorable Parts to Look For

- The parable of the yachtsman
- Humanity's double spiritual need

Introduction: In Defence of Everything Else

The only possible excuse for this book is that it is an answer to a challenge. Even a bad shot is dignified when he accepts a duel.

When some time ago I published a series of hasty but sincere papers, under the name of *Heretics,* several critics for whose intellect I have a warm respect (I may mention specially Mr. G. S. Street[1]) said that it was all very well for me to tell everybody to affirm his cosmic theory, but that I had carefully avoided supporting my precepts with example. "I will begin to worry about my philosophy," said Mr. Street, "when Mr. Chesterton has given us his."[2] It was perhaps

---

[1] George Slythe Street (1867–1936) was a British journalist and novelist, best known for his 1894 novel *The Autobiography of a Boy.*

[2] In the June 17, 1905, edition of the *Outlook,* Street's article "Mr. Chesterton" praised *Heretics* as a book with a thousand ideas, "a feast indeed . . . for a mind which loves ideas," revealing Chesterton as "an intellectual acrobat" who is, at times, "over-anxious to astonish" with his reliance on paradox. Street's biggest critique was that in *Heretics,* Chesterton's doctrine is "vague." He wrote: "That would not signify if he did not insist that a man's doctrine is the most important thing about him—I do not believe it—and

an incautious suggestion to make to a person only too ready to write books upon the feeblest provocation. But after all, though Mr. Street has inspired and created this book, he need not read it. If he does read it, he will find that in its pages I have attempted in a vague and personal way, in a set of mental pictures rather than in a series of deductions, to state the philosophy in which I have come to believe. I will not call it my philosophy; for I did not make it. God and humanity made it; and it made me.

The Man in the Yacht

I have often had a fancy for writing a romance about an English yachtsman who slightly miscalculated his course and discovered England under the impression that it was a new island in the South Seas. I always find, however, that I am either too busy or too lazy to write this fine work, so I may as well give it away for the purposes of philosophical illustration.

There will probably be a general impression that the man who landed (armed to the teeth and talking by signs) to plant the British flag on that barbaric temple which turned out to be the Pavilion at Brighton,[3] felt rather a fool. I am not here concerned to deny that he looked a fool. But if you imagine that he felt a fool, or at any rate that the sense of folly was his sole or his dominant emotion, then you have not studied with sufficient delicacy the rich romantic

---

that the fault of the age is its lack of doctrine. But he is always so insisting, and all I can gather of his own doctrine is his belief that everyone else ought to have one. I shall not begin to worry about my philosophy of life until Mr. Chesterton discloses his." This was the challenge that prompted Chesterton to write *Orthodoxy*.

[3] The Brighton Pavilion is a former royal residence located in Brighton, England, built in 1784 as a seaside retreat for George, Prince of Wales, who became King George IV in 1820. Chesterton might have chosen this place for the yachtsman's "discovery" because of its Indo-Saracenic style, with domes and minarets that were the work of architect John Nash.

nature of the hero of this tale. His mistake was really a most enviable mistake; and he knew it, if he was the man I take him for.

What could be more delightful than to have in the same few minutes all the fascinating terrors of going abroad combined with all the humane security of coming home again?

What could be better than to have all the fun of discovering South Africa without the disgusting necessity of landing there?

What could be more glorious than to brace one's self up to discover New South Wales and then realize, with a gush of happy tears, that it was really old South Wales.

Answering a Double Spiritual Need

This at least seems to me the main problem for philosophers, and is in a manner the main problem of this book. How can we contrive to be at once astonished at the world and yet at home in it? How can this queer cosmic town, with its many-legged citizens, with its monstrous and ancient lamps, how can this world give us at once the fascination of a strange town and the comfort and honour of being our own town?

To show that a faith or a philosophy is true from every standpoint would be too big an undertaking even for a much bigger book than this; it is necessary to follow one path of argument; and this is the path that I here propose to follow. I wish to set forth my faith as particularly answering this double spiritual need, the need for that mixture of the familiar and the unfamiliar which Christendom has rightly named romance. For the very word "romance" has in it the mystery and ancient meaning of Rome.

Any one setting out to dispute anything ought always to begin by saying what he does not dispute. Beyond stating what he proposes to prove, he should always state what he does not propose to prove. The thing I do not propose to prove, the thing I propose to take as common ground between myself and any average reader, is this desirability of an active and imaginative life, picturesque and full of a poetical curiosity, a life such as western man at any rate always seems to have desired. If a man says that extinction is better than existence or blank existence better than variety and adventure, then he is not one of the ordinary people to whom I am talking. If a man prefers nothing I can give him nothing. But nearly all people I have ever met in this western society in which I live would agree to the general proposition that we need this life of practical romance; the combination of something that is strange with something that is secure. We need so to view the world as to combine an idea of wonder and an idea of welcome. We need to be happy in this wonderland without once being merely comfortable. It is *this* achievement of my creed that I shall chiefly pursue in these pages.

My Discovery of Orthodoxy

But I have a peculiar reason for mentioning the man in a yacht, who discovered England. For I am that man in a yacht. I discovered England.

I do not see how this book can avoid being egotistical; and I do not quite see (to tell the truth) how it can avoid being dull. Dullness will, however, free me from the charge which I most lament; the charge of being flippant. Mere light sophistry is the thing that I happen to despise most of all things, and it is perhaps a wholesome fact that this is the thing of which I am generally accused. I know nothing so contemptible as a mere paradox; a mere ingenious defence of the indefensible.

If it were true (as has been said) that Mr. Bernard Shaw lived upon paradox,[4] then he ought to be a mere common millionaire;

---

[4] George Bernard Shaw (1856–1950), an Irish playwright, critic, and political activist, was Chesterton's most famous philosophical opponent. Chesterton wrote a book on Shaw in 1909, which opened with the statement: "Most people say that they agree with Bernard Shaw or that they do not understand him. I am the only person who understands him, and I do not agree with him." Despite the stark differences in their beliefs, Chesterton and Shaw were good friends with genuine affection for each other. Shaw said Chesterton was a "colossal genius."

for a man of his mental activity could invent a sophistry every six minutes. It is as easy as lying; because it is lying. The truth is, of course, that Mr. Shaw is cruelly hampered by the fact that he cannot tell any lie unless he thinks it is the truth. I find myself under the same intolerable bondage. I never in my life said anything merely because I thought it funny; though of course, I have had ordinary human vainglory, and may have thought it funny because I had said it. It is one thing to describe an interview with a gorgon or a griffin, a creature who does not exist. It is another thing to discover that the rhinoceros does exist and then take pleasure in the fact that he looks as if he didn't. One searches for truth, but it may be that one pursues instinctively the more extraordinary truths. And I offer this book with the heartiest sentiments to all the jolly people who hate what I write, and regard it (very justly, for all I know), as a piece of poor clowning or a single tiresome joke.

For if this book is a joke it is a joke against me. I am the man who with the utmost daring discovered what had been discovered before. If there is an element of farce in what follows, the farce is at my own expense; for this book explains how I fancied I was the first to set foot in Brighton and then found I was the last. It recounts my elephantine adventures in pursuit of the obvious. No one can think my case more ludicrous than I think it myself; no reader can accuse me here of trying to make a fool of him: I am the fool of this story, and no rebel shall hurl me from my throne.

I freely confess all the idiotic ambitions of the end of the nineteenth century. I did, like all other solemn little boys, try to be in advance of the age. Like them I tried to be some ten minutes in advance of the truth. And I found that I was eighteen hundred years behind it. I did strain my voice with a painfully juvenile exaggeration in uttering my truths. And I was punished in the fittest and funniest way, for I have kept my truths: but I have discovered, not that they were not truths, but simply that they were not mine. When I fancied that I stood alone I was really in the ridiculous position of being backed up by all Christendom. It may be, Heaven forgive me, that I did try to be original; but I only succeeded in inventing all by myself an inferior copy of the existing traditions of civilized religion.

The man from the yacht thought he was the first to find England; I thought I was the first to find Europe. I did try to found a heresy of my own; and when I had put the last touches to it, I discovered that it was orthodoxy.

The Meaning of "Orthodoxy"

It may be that somebody will be entertained by the account of this happy fiasco. It might amuse a friend or an enemy to read how I gradually learnt from the truth of some stray legend or from the falsehood of some dominant philosophy, things that I might have learnt from my catechism—if I had ever learnt it. There may or may not be some entertainment in reading how I found at last in an anarchist club or a Babylonian temple what I might have found in the nearest parish church. If any one is entertained by learning how the flowers of the field or the phrases in an omnibus, the accidents of politics or the pains of youth came together in a certain order to produce a certain conviction of Christian orthodoxy, he may possibly read this book. But there is in everything a reasonable division of labour. I have written the book, and nothing on earth would induce me to read it.

I add one purely pedantic note which comes, as a note naturally should, at the beginning of the book. These essays are concerned only to discuss the actual fact that the central Christian theology (sufficiently summarized in the Apostles' Creed) is the best root of energy and sound ethics. They are not intended to discuss the very fascinating but quite different question of what is the present seat of authority for the proclamation of that creed. When the word "orthodoxy" is used here it means the Apostles' Creed, as understood by everybody calling himself Christian until a very short time ago and the general historic conduct of those who held such a creed. I have been forced by mere space to confine myself to what I have got from this creed; I do not touch the matter much disputed among modern Christians, of where we ourselves got it. This is not an ecclesiastical treatise but a sort of slovenly autobiography. But if any one wants my opinions about the actual nature of the authority, Mr. G. S. Street has only to throw me another challenge, and I will write him another book.

Chapter Summary

In this introduction Chesterton compared himself to a yachtsman who set sail for foreign lands only to succeed in discovering his homeland. When Chesterton set out to create a philosophy that aligned with what he saw as common sense in the world, he found to his surprise that Christianity had discovered these truths long before him.

What is the philosophical conundrum that Chesterton seeks to resolve in the book? Put simply, it is the double spiritual need: finding the world both familiar and unfamiliar—to wonder at the world while feeling welcome in it. "How can we contrive to be at once astonished at the world and yet at home in it?"

The rest of the book seeks to answer this question, not as an apologetic in the classic sense, but as an intellectual autobiography. Chesterton will tell of his discovery of orthodoxy through a series of mental images, not through a systematician's approach. Chesterton has on his artist's cap, and he plans to paint a series of pictures that helps us see why humanity feels both the instinct of wonder at the world and the need for security and comfort in it, and why Christianity alone satisfies this double need.

Discussion Questions

1. What do you think of Chesterton's comment that he is not the maker of the Christian creed but that the Christian creed is what makes him?
2. In what ways do you feel "at home" and "welcome" in the world? In what ways do you feel uncomfortable or "astounded" at the world?
3. What mental images and associations are stirred up in you by the word "orthodoxy" in relation to Christianity? Are they positive or negative, or somewhere in between? Where do you think these associations come from?

TWO

For readers new to Chesterton, this chapter and the following are the most challenging parts of *Orthodoxy*. Chesterton begins his intellectual journey with a survey of contemporary thinking; many of the writers and philosophers and politicians he interacts with are now largely forgotten. What's more, Chesterton refers regularly to obscure figures and events from the past. To learn something about all the people he mentions would be an education in itself, even if you were to fail to follow his train of thought. In order to help the first-time reader, I've added multiple notes that give context to the people and places mentioned by Chesterton.

Chesterton's goal in this chapter is to begin the journey not with the reality of sin (which is what he and ancient philosophers would prefer) but with the question of sanity. Chesterton starts here because people may debate today whether or not you can lose your soul, but virtually no one debates that you can lose your mind. He seeks to demonstrate how the philosophies in his day resemble the circular, logical nature of people who have lost their wits. He argues that what is needed is not more *reason* but *mysticism*—a proper embrace of the mystery of the cosmos.

Memorable Parts to Look For

- The illustration of the insane asylum as the end result of contemporary thought

- "The clean and well-lit prison of one idea"
- The cramped universe of the one who "believes in himself"
- The symbolism of the circle and the cross

The Maniac

Thoroughly worldly people never understand even the world; they rely altogether on a few cynical maxims which are not true.

Once I remember walking with a prosperous publisher, who made a remark which I had often heard before; it is, indeed, almost a motto of the modern world. Yet I had heard it once too often, and I saw suddenly that there was nothing in it. The publisher said of somebody, "That man will get on; he believes in himself." And I remember that as I lifted my head to listen, my eye caught an omnibus on which was written "Hanwell."[1]

I said to him, "Shall I tell you where the men are who believe most in themselves? For I can tell you. I know of men who believe in themselves more colossally than Napoleon or Caesar. I know where flames the fixed star of certainty and success. I can guide you to the thrones of the Super-men. The men who really believe in themselves are all in lunatic asylums." He said mildly that there were a good many men after all who believed in themselves and who were not in lunatic asylums.

---

[1] Hanwell is short for Hanwell Insane Asylum (also known as Hanwell Pauper and Lunatic Asylum) in London. Some of the original buildings now make up the headquarters for the West London Mental Health NHS Trust.

"Yes, there are," I retorted, "and you of all men ought to know them. That drunken poet from whom you would not take a dreary tragedy, he believed in himself. That elderly minister with an epic from whom you were hiding in a back room, he believed in himself. If you consulted your business experience instead of your ugly individualistic philosophy, you would know that believing in himself is one of the commonest signs of a rotter. Actors who can't act believe in themselves; and debtors who won't pay. It would be much truer to say that a man will certainly fail, because he believes in himself. Complete self-confidence is not merely a sin; complete self-confidence is a weakness. Believing utterly in one's self is a hysterical and superstitious belief like believing in Joanna Southcote:[2] the man who has it has 'Hanwell' written on his face as plain as it is written on that omnibus."

And, to all this, my friend the publisher made this very deep and effective reply, "Well, if a man is not to believe in himself, in what is he to believe?"

After a long pause I replied, "I will go home and write a book in answer to that question." This is the book that I have written in answer to it.

Sin as a Starting Point?

But I think this book may well start where our argument started—in the neighbourhood of the mad-house. Modern masters of science are much impressed with the need of beginning all inquiry with a fact. The ancient masters of religion were quite equally impressed with that necessity. They began with the fact of sin—a fact as practical as potatoes. Whether or no man could be washed in miraculous waters, there was no doubt at any rate that he wanted washing.

---

[2] Joanna Southcote (also spelled Southcott) (1750–1814) was a self-proclaimed religious prophetess. A movement of "Southcottians" given to superstition grew in the years following her death, and interest in some of her prophecies lingered well into the twentieth century.

But certain religious leaders in London, not mere materialists,[3] have begun in our day not to deny the highly disputable water, but to deny the indisputable dirt. Certain new theologians dispute original sin,[4] which is the only part of Christian theology which can really be proved. Some followers of the Reverend R. J. Campbell,[5] in their almost too fastidious spirituality, admit divine sinlessness, which they cannot see even in their dreams. But they essentially deny human sin, which they can see in the street.

The strongest saints and the strongest sceptics alike took positive evil as the starting-point of their argument. If it be true (as it certainly is) that a man can feel exquisite happiness in skinning a cat, then the religious philosopher can only draw one of two deductions. He must either deny the existence of God, as all atheists do; or he must deny the present union between God and man, as all Christians do. The new theologians seem to think it a highly rationalistic solution to deny the cat.

Sanity as the Starting Point

In this remarkable situation it is plainly not now possible (with any hope of a universal appeal) to start, as our fathers did, with the fact of sin. This very fact which was to them (and is to me) as plain as a pikestaff, is the very fact that has been specially diluted or denied. But though moderns deny the existence of sin, I do not think that

---

[3] When Chesterton refers to "materialists" in this book, he does not convey the modern understanding of "materialistic"—someone preoccupied with his or her possessions or wealth. "Materialists" and "materialism" refer to the naturalist philosophy that this world—the world of matter—is all there is, in opposition to those who believe in God or in the supernatural (including the possibility of miracles).

[4] The doctrine of "original sin" refers to the condition of sinfulness that has marked humanity since Adam and Eve.

[5] Reginald John Campbell (1867–1956) was a popular preacher and leading exponent of "The New Theology," a movement that sought to harmonize Christianity with contemporary views and beliefs.

they have yet denied the existence of a lunatic asylum. We all agree still that there is a collapse of the intellect as unmistakable as a falling house. Men deny hell, but not, as yet, Hanwell. For the purpose of our primary argument the one may very well stand where the other stood. I mean that as all thoughts and theories were once judged by whether they tended to make a man lose his soul, so for our present purpose all modern thoughts and theories may be judged by whether they tend to make a man lose his wits.

It is true that some speak lightly and loosely of insanity as in itself attractive. But a moment's thought will show that if disease is beautiful, it is generally someone else's disease. A blind man may be picturesque; but it requires two eyes to see the picture. And similarly even the wildest poetry of insanity can only be enjoyed by the sane. To the insane man his insanity is quite prosaic, because it is quite true. A man who thinks himself a chicken is to himself as ordinary as a chicken. A man who thinks he is a bit of glass is to himself as dull as a bit of glass. It is the homogeneity of his mind which makes him dull, and which makes him mad. It is only because we see the irony of his idea that we think him even amusing; it is only because he does not see the irony of his idea that he is put in Hanwell at all.

In short, oddities only strike ordinary people. Oddities do not strike odd people. This is why ordinary people have a much more exciting time; while odd people are always complaining of the dullness of life. This is also why the new novels die so quickly, and why the old fairy tales endure forever. The old fairy tale makes the hero a normal human boy; it is his adventures that are startling; they startle him because he is normal. But in the modern psychological novel the hero is abnormal; the centre is not central. Hence the fiercest adventures fail to affect him adequately, and the book is monotonous. You can make a story out of a hero among dragons; but not out of a dragon among dragons. The fairy tale discusses what a sane man will do in a mad world. The sober realistic novel of today discusses what an essential lunatic will do in a dull world.

The Imagination Is Indispensable to Sanity

Let us begin, then, with the mad-house; from this evil and fantastic inn let us set forth on our intellectual journey.

Now, if we are to glance at the philosophy of sanity, the first thing to do in the matter is to blot out one big and common mistake. There is a notion adrift everywhere that imagination, especially mystical imagination, is dangerous to man's mental balance. Poets are commonly spoken of as psychologically unreliable; and generally there is a vague association between wreathing laurels in your hair and sticking straws in it. Facts and history utterly contradict this view. Most of the very great poets have been not only sane, but extremely business-like; and if Shakespeare ever really held horses, it was because he was much the safest man to hold them.

Imagination does not breed insanity. Exactly what does breed insanity is reason. Poets do not go mad; but chess-players do. Mathematicians go mad, and cashiers; but creative artists very seldom. I am not, as will be seen, in any sense attacking logic: I only say that this danger does lie in logic, not in imagination. Artistic paternity is as wholesome as physical paternity.

Moreover, it is worthy of remark that when a poet really was morbid it was commonly because he had some weak spot of rationality on his brain. Poe,[6] for instance, really was morbid; not because he was poetical, but because he was specially analytical. Even chess was too poetical for him; he disliked chess because it was full of knights and castles, like a poem. He avowedly preferred the black discs of draughts,[7] because they were more like the mere black dots on a diagram.

Perhaps the strongest case of all is this: that only one great English poet went mad, Cowper.[8] And he was definitely driven mad

---

[6] Edgar Allan Poe (1809–49), an American writer best known for his poetry and short stories, which often focused on mystery and the macabre.

[7] The British name for the game of checkers.

[8] William Cowper (1731–1800), an English poet and composer of hymns, most notably "God Moves in a Mysterious Way." John Newton (author of

by logic, by the ugly and alien logic of predestination.[9] Poetry was not the disease, but the medicine; poetry partly kept him in health. He could sometimes forget the red and thirsty hell to which his hideous necessitarianism dragged him among the wide waters and the white flat lilies of the Ouse.[10] He was damned by John Calvin;[11] he was almost saved by John Gilpin.[12]

Everywhere we see that men do not go mad by dreaming. Critics are much madder than poets. Homer is complete and calm enough; it is his critics who tear him into extravagant tatters. Shakespeare is quite himself; it is only some of his critics who have discovered that he was somebody else. And though St. John the Evangelist saw many strange monsters in his vision,[13] he saw no creature so wild as one of his own commentators.

The general fact is simple. Poetry is sane because it floats easily in an infinite sea; reason seeks to cross the infinite sea, and so make it finite. The result is mental exhaustion, like the physical exhaustion of Mr. Holbein.[14] To accept everything is an exercise, to understand everything a strain. The poet only desires exaltation and expansion, a world to stretch himself in. The poet only asks to get his head into the heavens. It is the logician who seeks to get the heavens into his head. And it is his head that splits.

"Amazing Grace") was a friend to Cowper and sought to encourage him when he experienced periods of profound depression and spiritual doubt.

[9] The doctrine of predestination as understood by Calvinists (God is the sole determiner of who receives salvation or damnation) during the time of the Puritans led many Christians of that era, including Cowper, to excessive introspection regarding their spiritual state.

[10] A river in North Yorkshire, England.

[11] John Calvin (1509–64), Protestant theologian known for an emphasis on the absolute sovereignty of God in salvation and damnation.

[12] John Gilpin was the subject in a well-known comic ballad by William Cowper in 1782, "The Diverting History of John Gilpin."

[13] As recorded in Revelation, the last book of the Bible.

[14] Chesterton is likely referring to Hans Holbein the Younger (1497–1543), a German painter known for the meticulous finish of his portraits.

It is a small matter, but not irrelevant, that this striking mistake is commonly supported by a striking misquotation. We have all heard people cite the celebrated line of Dryden as "Great genius is to madness near allied."[15] But Dryden did not say that great genius was to madness near allied. Dryden was a great genius himself, and knew better. It would have been hard to find a man more romantic than he, or more sensible. What Dryden said was this, "Great wits are oft to madness near allied"; and that is true. It is the pure promptitude of the intellect that is in peril of a breakdown.

Also people might remember of what sort of man Dryden was talking. He was not talking of any unworldly visionary like Vaughan or George Herbert.[16] He was talking of a cynical man of the world, a sceptic, a diplomatist, a great practical politician. Such men are indeed to madness near allied. Their incessant calculation of their own brains and other people's brains is a dangerous trade. It is always perilous to the mind to reckon up the mind. A flippant person has asked why we say, "As mad as a hatter." A more flippant person might answer that a hatter is mad because he has to measure the human head.

The Logical Nature of Lunacy

And if great reasoners are often maniacal, it is equally true that maniacs are commonly great reasoners. When I was engaged in a controversy with the *Clarion* on the matter of free will, that able writer Mr. R. B. Suthers said that free will was lunacy,[17] because it meant causeless actions, and the actions of a lunatic would be causeless. I do not dwell here upon the disastrous lapse in determinist

---

[15] John Dryden (1631–1700) was made England's first poet laureate in 1668.

[16] Henry Vaughan (1621–95) was an author who wrote religious poetry. George Herbert (1593–1633) was a Welsh-born poet and priest, considered to be one of the greatest British devotional lyricists in history.

[17] Robert Bentley Suthers was a writer for the socialist newspaper the *Clarion* and a supporter of Robert Blatchford in his debate with Chesterton.

logic. Obviously if any actions, even a lunatic's, can be causeless, determinism is done for.[18] If the chain of causation can be broken for a madman, it can be broken for a man.

But my purpose is to point out something more practical. It was natural, perhaps, that a modern Marxian Socialist should not know anything about free will.[19] But it was certainly remarkable that a modern Marxian Socialist should not know anything about lunatics. Mr. Suthers evidently did not know anything about lunatics. The last thing that can be said of a lunatic is that his actions are causeless.

If any human acts may loosely be called causeless, they are the minor acts of a healthy man; whistling as he walks; slashing the grass with a stick; kicking his heels or rubbing his hands. It is the happy man who does the useless things; the sick man is not strong enough to be idle.

It is exactly such careless and causeless actions that the madman could never understand; for the madman (like the determinist) generally sees too much cause in everything. The madman would read a conspiratorial significance into those empty activities. He would think that the lopping of the grass was an attack on private property. He would think that the kicking of the heels was a signal to an accomplice. If the madman could for an instant become careless, he would become sane.

Everyone who has had the misfortune to talk with people in the heart or on the edge of mental disorder, knows that their most sinister quality is a horrible clarity of detail; a connecting of one thing with another in a map more elaborate than a maze. If you argue with a madman, it is extremely probable that you will get the worst of it; for in many ways his mind moves all the quicker for

---

[18] Determinism is the philosophical belief that human beings have no free will, since all events are ultimately determined by preexisting causes, all of which are external to the human will.

[19] Chesterton here is referring to those who follow Karl Marx's materialist assumptions.

not being delayed by the things that go with good judgment. He is not hampered by a sense of humour or by charity, or by the dumb certainties of experience. He is the more logical for losing certain sane affections. Indeed, the common phrase for insanity is in this respect a misleading one. The madman is not the man who has lost his reason. The madman is the man who has lost everything except his reason.

Three Cases of Madness

The madman's explanation of a thing is always complete, and often in a purely rational sense satisfactory. Or, to speak more strictly, the insane explanation, if not conclusive, is at least unanswerable; this may be observed specially in the two or three commonest kinds of madness.

(1) If a man says (for instance) that men have a conspiracy against him, you cannot dispute it except by saying that all the men deny that they are conspirators; which is exactly what conspirators would do. His explanation covers the facts as much as yours.

(2) Or if a man says that he is the rightful King of England, it is no complete answer to say that the existing authorities call him mad; for if he were King of England that might be the wisest thing for the existing authorities to do.

(3) Or if a man says that he is Jesus Christ, it is no answer to tell him that the world denies his divinity; for the world denied Christ's.

Nevertheless he is wrong. But if we attempt to trace his error in exact terms, we shall not find it quite so easy as we had supposed.

Perhaps the nearest we can get to expressing it is to say this: that his mind moves in a perfect but narrow circle. A small circle is quite as infinite as a large circle; but, though it is quite as infinite, it is not so large. In the same way the insane explanation is quite as complete as the sane one, but it is not so large. A bullet is quite as round as the world, but it is not the world. There is such a thing as a narrow universality; there is such a thing as a small and cramped eternity; you may see it in many modern religions.

Now, speaking quite externally and empirically, we may say that the strongest and most unmistakable *mark* of madness is this combination between a logical completeness and a spiritual contraction. The lunatic's theory explains a large number of things, but it does not explain them in a large way. I mean that if you or I were dealing with a mind that was growing morbid, we should be chiefly concerned not so much to give it arguments as to give it air, to convince it that there was something cleaner and cooler outside the suffocation of a single argument.

(1) Suppose, for instance, it were the first case that I took as typical; suppose it were the case of a man who accused everybody of conspiring against him. If we could express our deepest feelings of protest and appeal against this obsession, I suppose we should say something like this: "Oh, I admit that you have your case and have it by heart, and that many things do fit into other things as you say. I admit that your explanation explains a great deal; but what a great deal it leaves out! Are there no other stories in the world except yours; and are all men busy with your business? Suppose we grant the details; perhaps when the man in the street did not seem to see you it was only his cunning; perhaps when the policeman asked you your name it was only because he knew it already. But how much happier you would be if you only knew that these people cared nothing about you! How much larger your life would be if your self could become smaller in it; if you could really look at other men with common curiosity and pleasure; if you could see them walking as they are in their sunny selfishness and their virile indifference! You would begin to be interested in them, because they were not interested in you. You would break out of this tiny and tawdry theatre in which your own little plot is always being played, and you would find yourself under a freer sky, in a street full of splendid strangers."

(2) Or suppose it were the second case of madness, that of a man who claims the crown, your impulse would be to answer, "All right! Perhaps you know that you are the King of England; but why do you care? Make one magnificent effort and you will be a human being and look down on all the kings of the earth."

(3) Or it might be the third case, of the madman who called himself Christ. If we said what we felt, we should say, "So you are the Creator and Redeemer of the world: but what a small world it must be! What a little heaven you must inhabit, with angels no bigger than butterflies! How sad it must be to be God; and an inadequate God! Is there really no life fuller and no love more marvellous than yours; and is it really in your small and painful pity that all flesh must put its faith? How much happier you would be, how much more of you there would be, if the hammer of a higher God could smash your small cosmos, scattering the stars like spangles, and leave you in the open, free like other men to look up as well as down!"

And it must be remembered that the most purely practical science does take this view of mental evil; it does not seek to argue with it like a heresy but simply to snap it like a spell.

The Prison of One Idea

Neither modern science nor ancient religion believes in complete free thought. Theology rebukes certain thoughts by calling them blasphemous. Science rebukes certain thoughts by calling them morbid.

For example, some religious societies discouraged men more or less from thinking about sex. The new scientific society definitely discourages men from thinking about death; it is a fact, but it is considered a morbid fact. And in dealing with those whose morbidity has a touch of mania, modern science cares far less for pure logic than a dancing Dervish.[20] In these cases it is not enough that the unhappy man should desire truth; he must desire health. Nothing can save him but a blind hunger for normality, like that of a beast.

A man cannot think himself out of mental evil; for it is actually the organ of thought that has become diseased, ungovernable,

[20] A member of a Muslim ascetic order, known for performing whirling dances and vigorous chanting. Also refers more generally to people with abundant, frenzied energy.

and, as it were, independent. He can only be saved by will or faith. The moment his mere reason moves, it moves in the old circular rut; he will go round and round his logical circle, just as a man in a third-class carriage on the Inner Circle will go round and round the Inner Circle unless he performs the voluntary, vigorous, and mystical act of getting out at Gower Street.[21]

Decision is the whole business here; a door must be shut forever. Every remedy is a desperate remedy. Every cure is a miraculous cure. Curing a madman is not arguing with a philosopher; it is casting out a devil. And however quietly doctors and psychologists may go to work in the matter, their attitude is profoundly intolerant—as intolerant as Bloody Mary.[22] Their attitude is really this: that the man must stop thinking, if he is to go on living. Their counsel is one of intellectual amputation. If thy *head* offend thee, cut it off; for it is better, not merely to enter the Kingdom of Heaven as a child, but to enter it as an imbecile, rather than with your whole intellect to be cast into hell—or into Hanwell.[23]

Such is the madman of experience; he is commonly a reasoner, frequently a successful reasoner. Doubtless he could be vanquished in mere reason, and the case against him put logically. But it can be put much more precisely in more general and even aesthetic terms. He is in the clean and well-lit prison of one idea: he is sharpened to one painful point. He is without healthy hesitation and healthy complexity.

---

[21] The Inner Circle is a London underground line in a spiraling shape, now known as the Circle Line.

[22] Queen Mary I of England was notorious for her attempts to reverse the Protestant Reformation, leading to more than 280 dissenters being burned at the stake.

[23] Chesterton's comment is a twist on Jesus's saying in Matt 5:30: "And if thy right hand offend thee, cut it off, and cast it from thee: for it is profitable for thee that one of thy members should perish, and not that thy whole body should be cast into hell."

The Mania of Modern Thinking

Now, as I explain in the introduction, I have determined in these early chapters to give not so much a diagram of a doctrine as some pictures of a point of view. And I have described at length my vision of the maniac for this reason: that just as I am affected by the maniac, so I am affected by most modern thinkers. That unmistakable mood or note that I hear from Hanwell, I hear also from half the chairs of science and seats of learning today; and most of the mad doctors are mad doctors in more senses than one. They all have exactly that combination we have noted: the combination of an expansive and exhaustive reason with a contracted common sense. They are universal only in the sense that they take one thin explanation and carry it very far. But a pattern can stretch forever and still be a small pattern. They see a chessboard white on black, and if the universe is paved with it, it is still white on black. Like the lunatic, they cannot alter their standpoint; they cannot make a mental effort and suddenly see it black on white.

The Madness of Materialism

Take first the more obvious case of materialism. As an explanation of the world, materialism has a sort of insane simplicity. It has just the quality of the madman's argument; we have at once the sense of it covering everything and the sense of it leaving everything out.

Contemplate some able and sincere materialist, as, for instance, Mr. McCabe,[24] and you will have exactly this unique sensation. He understands everything, and everything does not seem worth understanding. His cosmos may be complete in every rivet and cogwheel, but still his cosmos is smaller than our world. Somehow his

[24] Joseph Martin McCabe (1867–1955) left the priesthood and became a writer devoted to rationalism and freethought. He was an opponent of Chesterton in the debate that unfolded in the *Clarion*, and Chesterton devoted a chapter to critiquing McCabe's philosophy in *Heretics*.

scheme, like the lucid scheme of the madman, seems unconscious of the alien energies and the large indifference of the earth; it is not thinking of the real things of the earth, of fighting peoples or proud mothers, or first love or fear upon the sea. The earth is so very large, and the cosmos is so very small. The cosmos is about the smallest hole that a man can hide his head in.

It must be understood that I am not now discussing the relation of these creeds to truth; but, for the present, solely their relation to health. Later in the argument I hope to attack the question of objective verity; here I speak only of a phenomenon of psychology. I do not for the present attempt to prove to Haeckel that materialism is untrue,[25] any more than I attempted to prove to the man who thought he was Christ that he was labouring under an error. I merely remark here on the fact that both cases have the same kind of completeness and the same kind of incompleteness. You can explain a man's detention at Hanwell by an indifferent public by saying that it is the crucifixion of a god of whom the world is not worthy. The explanation does explain. Similarly you may explain the order in the universe by saying that all things, even the souls of men, are leaves inevitably unfolding on an utterly unconscious tree—the blind destiny of matter. The explanation does explain, though not, of course, so completely as the madman's.

But the point here is that the normal human mind not only objects to both, but feels to both the same objection. Its approximate statement is that if the man in Hanwell is the real God, he is not much of a god. And, similarly, if the cosmos of the materialist is the real cosmos, it is not much of a cosmos. The thing has shrunk. The deity is less divine than many men; and (according to Haeckel) the whole of life is something much more grey, narrow, and trivial than many separate aspects of it. The parts seem greater than the whole.

---

[25] Ernst Haeckel (1834–1919), German zoologist and naturalist philosopher who believed there is no immortal soul, free will, or personal God.

For we must remember that the materialist philosophy (whether true or not) is certainly much more limiting than any religion. In one sense, of course, all intelligent ideas are narrow. They cannot be broader than themselves. A Christian is only restricted in the same sense that an atheist is restricted. He cannot think Christianity false and continue to be a Christian; and the atheist cannot think atheism false and continue to be an atheist.

But as it happens, there is a very special sense in which materialism has more restrictions than spiritualism. Mr. McCabe thinks me a slave because I am not allowed to believe in determinism. I think Mr. McCabe a slave because he is not allowed to believe in fairies. But if we examine the two vetoes we shall see that his is really much more of a pure veto than mine. The Christian is quite free to believe that there is a considerable amount of settled order and inevitable development in the universe. But the materialist is not allowed to admit into his spotless machine the slightest speck of spiritualism or miracle. Poor Mr. McCabe is not allowed to retain even the tiniest imp, though it might be hiding in a pimpernel.

The Christian admits that the universe is manifold and even miscellaneous, just as a sane man knows that he is complex. The sane man knows that he has a touch of the beast, a touch of the devil, a touch of the saint, a touch of the citizen. Nay, the really sane man knows that he has a touch of the madman. But the materialist's world is quite simple and solid, just as the madman is quite sure he is sane. The materialist is sure that history has been simply and solely a chain of causation, just as the interesting person before mentioned is quite sure that he is simply and solely a chicken. Materialists and madmen never have doubts.

Spiritual doctrines do not actually limit the mind as do materialistic denials. Even if I believe in immortality I need not think about it. But if I disbelieve in immortality I must not think about it. In the first case the road is open and I can go as far as I like; in the second the road is shut.

Materialism and Fatalism

But the case is even stronger, and the parallel with madness is yet more strange. For it was our case against the exhaustive and logical theory of the lunatic that, right or wrong, it gradually destroyed his humanity. Now it is the charge against the main deductions of the materialist that, right or wrong, they gradually destroy his humanity; I do not mean only kindness, I mean hope, courage, poetry, initiative, all that is human.

For instance, when materialism leads men to complete fatalism (as it generally does), it is quite idle to pretend that it is in any sense a liberating force. It is absurd to say that you are especially advancing freedom when you only use free thought to destroy free will. The determinists come to bind, not to loose. They may well call their law the "chain" of causation. It is the worst chain that ever fettered a human being. You may use the language of liberty, if you like, about materialistic teaching, but it is obvious that this is just as inapplicable to it as a whole as the same language when applied to a man locked up in a mad-house. You may say, if you like, that the man is free to think himself a poached egg. But it is surely a more massive and important fact that if he is a poached egg, he is not free to eat, drink, sleep, walk, or smoke a cigarette. Similarly you may say, if you like, that the bold determinist speculator is free to disbelieve in the reality of the will. But it is a much more massive and important fact that he is not free to raise, to curse, to thank, to justify, to urge, to punish, to resist temptations, to incite mobs, to make New Year resolutions, to pardon sinners, to rebuke tyrants, or even to say "thank you" for the mustard.

The Effect of Materialism and Determinism on Mercy

In passing from this subject I may note that there is a queer fallacy to the effect that materialistic fatalism is in some way favourable to mercy, to the abolition of cruel punishments or punishments of any kind. This is startlingly the reverse of the truth. It is quite tenable that the doctrine of necessity makes no difference at all; that it leaves the flogger flogging and the kind friend exhorting as before. But obviously if it stops either of them, it stops the kind exhortation. That the sins are inevitable does not prevent punishment; if it prevents anything it prevents persuasion.

Determinism is quite as likely to lead to cruelty as it is certain to lead to cowardice. Determinism is not inconsistent with the cruel treatment of criminals. What it is (perhaps) inconsistent with is the generous treatment of criminals; with any appeal to their better feelings or encouragement in their moral struggle. The determinist does not believe in appealing to the will, but he does believe in changing the environment. He must not say to the sinner, "Go and sin no more,"[26] because the sinner cannot help it. But he can put him in boiling oil; for boiling oil is an environment. Considered as a figure, therefore, the materialist has the fantastic outline of the figure of the madman. Both take up a position at once unanswerable and intolerable.

The Madness of Self-Centered Scepticism

Of course it is not only of the materialist that all this is true. The same would apply to the other extreme of speculative logic.

There is a sceptic far more terrible than he who believes that everything began in matter. It is possible to meet the sceptic who believes that everything began in himself. He doubts not the existence of angels or devils, but the existence of men and cows. For him his own friends are a mythology made up by himself. He created his own father and his own mother. This horrible fancy has in it something decidedly attractive to the somewhat mystical egoism of our day. That publisher who thought that men would get on if they believed in themselves, those seekers after the Superman who

[26] The words of Jesus to a woman caught in adultery (John 8:11).

are always looking for him in the looking-glass,[27] those writers who talk about impressing their personalities instead of creating life for the world, all these people have really only an inch between them and this awful emptiness. Then when this kindly world all round the man has been blackened out like a lie; when friends fade into ghosts, and the foundations of the world fail; then when the man, believing in nothing and in no man, is alone in his own nightmare, then the great individualistic motto shall be written over him in avenging irony. The stars will be only dots in the blackness of his own brain; his mother's face will be only a sketch from his own insane pencil on the walls of his cell. But over his cell shall be written, with dreadful truth, "He believes in himself."

All that concerns us here, however, is to note that this panegoistic extreme of thought exhibits the same paradox as the other extreme of materialism.[28] It is equally complete in theory and equally crippling in practice.

For the sake of simplicity, it is easier to state the notion by saying that a man can believe that he is always in a dream. Now, obviously there can be no positive proof given to him that he is not in a dream, for the simple reason that no proof can be offered that might not be offered in a dream. But if the man began to burn down London and say that his housekeeper would soon call him to breakfast, we should take him and put him with other logicians in a place which has often been alluded to in the course of this chapter. The man who cannot believe his senses, and the man who cannot believe anything else, are both insane, but their insanity is proved not by any error in their argument, but by the manifest mistake of their whole lives. They have both locked themselves up in two boxes, painted inside with the sun and stars; they are both unable to get out, the one into the health and happiness of heaven, the other even into the health and happiness of the earth. Their

---

[27] By "Superman," Chesterton is referring to a term used by Friedrich Nietzsche, "the superior man" who justifies the existence of the human race.

[28] Panegoism is a form of philosophical skepticism.

position is quite reasonable; nay, in a sense it is infinitely reasonable, just as a threepenny bit is infinitely circular.[29]

But there is such a thing as a mean infinity, a base and slavish eternity. It is amusing to notice that many of the moderns, whether sceptics or mystics, have taken as their sign a certain eastern symbol, which is the very symbol of this ultimate nullity. When they wish to represent eternity, they represent it by a serpent with his tail in his mouth. There is a startling sarcasm in the image of that very unsatisfactory meal. The eternity of the material fatalists, the eternity of the eastern pessimists, the eternity of the supercilious theosophists and higher scientists of today is, indeed, very well presented by a serpent eating his tail, a degraded animal who destroys even himself.

The Requirement of Mysticism for Sanity

This chapter is purely practical and is concerned with what actually is the chief mark and element of insanity; we may say in summary that it is reason used without root, reason in the void. The man who begins to think without the proper first principles goes mad; he begins to think at the wrong end. And for the rest of these pages we have to try and discover what is the right end.

But we may ask in conclusion, if this be what drives men mad, what is it that keeps them sane? By the end of this book I hope to give a definite, some will think a far too definite, answer. But for the moment it is possible in the same solely practical manner to give a general answer touching what in actual human history keeps men sane. Mysticism keeps men sane. As long as you have mystery you have health; when you destroy mystery you create morbidity.

The ordinary man has always been sane because the ordinary man has always been a mystic. He has permitted the twilight. He has always had one foot in earth and the other in fairyland. He has always left himself free to doubt his gods; but (unlike the agnostic of today)

[29] A threepenny bit was a British coin worth three pennies.

free also to believe in them. He has always cared more for truth than for consistency. If he saw two truths that seemed to contradict each other, he would take the two truths and the contradiction along with them. His spiritual sight is stereoscopic, like his physical sight: he sees two different pictures at once and yet sees all the better for that. Thus he has always believed that there was such a thing as fate, but such a thing as free will also. Thus he believed that children were indeed the kingdom of heaven, but nevertheless ought to be obedient to the kingdom of earth. He admired youth because it was young and age because it was not. It is exactly this balance of apparent contradictions that has been the whole buoyancy of the healthy man.

The whole secret of mysticism is this: that man can understand everything by the help of what he does not understand. The morbid logician seeks to make everything lucid, and succeeds in making everything mysterious. The mystic allows one thing to be mysterious, and everything else becomes lucid.

The determinist makes the theory of causation quite clear, and then finds that he cannot say "if you please" to the housemaid. The Christian permits free will to remain a sacred mystery; but because of this his relations with the housemaid become of a sparkling and crystal clearness. He puts the seed of dogma in a central darkness; but it branches forth in all directions with abounding natural health.

The Circle and the Cross

As we have taken the circle as the symbol of reason and madness, we may very well take the cross as the symbol at once of mystery and of health. Buddhism is centripetal, but Christianity is centrifugal: it breaks out. For the circle is perfect and infinite in its nature; but it is fixed forever in its size; it can never be larger or smaller. But the cross, though it has at its heart a collision and a contradiction, can extend its four arms forever without altering its shape. Because it has a paradox in its centre it can grow without changing. The circle returns upon itself and is bound. The cross opens its arms to the four winds; it is a signpost for free travellers.

Symbols alone are of even a cloudy value in speaking of this deep matter; and another symbol from physical nature will express sufficiently well the real place of mysticism before mankind. The one created thing which we cannot look at is the one thing in the light of which we look at everything. Like the sun at noonday, mysticism explains everything else by the blaze of its own victorious invisibility. Detached intellectualism is (in the exact sense of a popular phrase) all moonshine; for it is light without heat, and it is secondary light, reflected from a dead world. But the Greeks were right when they made Apollo the god both of imagination and of sanity; for he was both the patron of poetry and the patron of healing.

Of necessary dogmas and a special creed I shall speak later. But that transcendentalism by which all men live has primarily much the position of the sun in the sky. We are conscious of it as of a kind of splendid confusion; it is something both shining and shapeless, at once a blaze and a blur. But the circle of the moon is as clear and unmistakable, as recurrent and inevitable, as the circle of Euclid on a blackboard.[30] For the moon is utterly reasonable; and the moon is the mother of lunatics and has given to them all her name.

---

[30] Euclid of Alexandria, considered the "founder of geometry," was born in the mid-fourth century BC.

Chapter Summary

In this chapter Chesterton began his intellectual journey by demonstrating how the philosophies of his day resemble the tight, circular logic of people in mental institutions. Materialist philosophies, and the corresponding fatalism and determinism that follow, lead away from mental health and human happiness. So also does the scepticism associated with doubting the existence of everything except your mind and experience. Whether one believes the world is all there is, or himself to be all there is, the result is the same: a more restrictive and binding approach to life that minimizes the glory of the world and shrinks the self's capacity for human happiness.

What should be the response to these philosophies that lead to madness? One might expect Chesterton to appeal to reason based on logical argumentation as the way to sanity. Instead, Chesterton believed the answer is in mysticism—the embrace of the mystery. Sanity requires the imagination, not just logic. He contrasted the symbol of the circle, which no matter how large or small is always closed, with the symbol of the cross, which due to the sacred mystery of its apparent contradiction at the center can continue to break out and expand.

Discussion Questions

1. Why do you think Chesterton critiques the common phrase that one should "believe in himself"?
2. Why are both reason and imagination indispensable to sanity and happiness?
3. In what ways does a materialist philosophy limit the mind? What about a determinist philosophy?
4. What does Chesterton mean by "mysticism," and why does he believe it is so important to maintaining one's sanity?

THREE

Readers of *Orthodoxy* often tell me they find the third chapter most difficult. This would not have surprised Chesterton, for even he admits at the end that this is "the first and dullest business of this book." Here, Chesterton surveys the landscape of contemporary thought, interacting with philosophers and writers, while seeking to follow these paths of intellectual skepticism to their dead ends. As you read, you might wonder if Chesterton is reversing course in some way. After all, in chapter 2, he claimed reason wasn't enough to maintain sanity; we need the imagination. Now, in this chapter, he takes on the skeptic who wonders if we can really reason at all.

Chesterton's goal in this chapter is to defend reason by showing how contemporary thinkers—materialists, idealists, social Darwinists, and progressivists—reduce everything philosophically to a principle that, followed to its conclusion, destroys or prevents further thought. Recognizing the dead end of these reductionist philosophies, some thinkers turned to the ultimate authority of "the will," an important stage in Nietzsche's thought. Chesterton takes on the reductionist philosophies *and* those who would exalt the will above all else by showing that unless there are absolutes and first principles, there is nothing to fight about. And surprisingly, it is religious authority and its insistence on the need for faith that preserves us from these errors.

Memorable Parts to Look For

- The damage caused by Christian virtues let loose, disconnected from each other
- Chesterton's distinction between the old meaning of *humility* and the new
- The embrace of a world of limits, and the exercise of the will as an act of self-limitation
- Joan of Arc as a blazing path through the paralysis of living always at philosophical crossroads

The Suicide of Thought

The phrases of the street are not only forcible but subtle: for a figure of speech can often get into a crack too small for a definition. Phrases like "put out" or "off colour" might have been coined by Mr. Henry James in an agony of verbal precision.[1] And there is no more subtle truth than that of the everyday phrase about a man having "his heart in the right place." It involves the idea of normal proportion; not only does a certain function exist, but it is rightly related to other functions. Indeed, the negation of this phrase would describe with peculiar accuracy the somewhat morbid mercy and perverse tenderness of the most representative moderns. If, for instance, I had to describe with fairness the character of Mr. Bernard Shaw, I could not express myself more exactly than by saying that he has a heroically large and generous heart; but not a heart in the right place. And this is so of the typical society of our time.

The modern world is not evil; in some ways the modern world is far too good. It is full of wild and wasted virtues. When a religious scheme is shattered (as Christianity was shattered at the Reformation), it is not merely the vices that are let loose. The vices are, indeed, let loose, and they wander and do damage. But the

---

[1] Henry James (1843–1916) was an influential American novelist and brother of William James, the renowned philosopher and psychologist.

virtues are let loose also; and the virtues wander more wildly, and the virtues do more terrible damage.

The modern world is full of the old Christian virtues gone mad. The virtues have gone mad because they have been isolated from each other and are wandering alone. Thus some scientists care for truth; and their truth is pitiless. Thus some humanitarians only care for pity; and their pity (I am sorry to say) is often untruthful.

For example, Mr. Blatchford attacks Christianity because he is mad on one Christian virtue:[2] the merely mystical and almost irrational virtue of charity. He has a strange idea that he will make it easier to forgive sins by saying that there are no sins to forgive. Mr. Blatchford is not only an early Christian, he is the only early Christian who ought really to have been eaten by lions. For in his case the pagan accusation is really true: his mercy would mean mere anarchy. He really is the enemy of the human race—because he is so human.

As the other extreme, we may take the acrid realist, who has deliberately killed in himself all human pleasure in happy tales or in the healing of the heart. Torquemada tortured people physically for the sake of moral truth.[3] Zola tortured people morally for the sake of physical truth.[4] But in Torquemada's time there was at least a system that could to some extent make righteousness and peace kiss each other. Now they do not even bow. But a much stronger case than these two of truth and pity can be found in the remarkable case of the dislocation of humility.

---

[2] Robert Blatchford (1851–1943) was a socialist journalist and author in the United Kingdom. An atheist, he and Chesterton had a dispute over Christianity that lasted two years, with a series of articles in the *Clarion*.

[3] Tomás de Torquemada (1420–98) was the first Grand Inquisitor in Spain's quest to suppress heresy.

[4] Émile Zola (1840–1902) was a French novelist and the best-known practitioner of the literary school of naturalism. He saw people as products of their environment.

The Changing Meaning of "Humility"

It is only with one aspect of humility that we are here concerned. Humility was largely meant as a restraint upon the arrogance and infinity of the appetite of man. He was always outstripping his mercies with his own newly invented needs. His very power of enjoyment destroyed half his joys. By asking for pleasure, he lost the chief pleasure; for the chief pleasure is surprise. Hence it became evident that if a man would make his world large, he must be always making himself small. Even the haughty visions, the tall cities, and the toppling pinnacles are the creations of humility. Giants that tread down forests like grass are the creations of humility. Towers that vanish upwards above the loneliest star are the creations of humility. For towers are not tall unless we look up at them; and giants are not giants unless they are larger than we. All this gigantesque imagination, which is, perhaps, the mightiest of the pleasures of man, is at bottom entirely humble. It is impossible without humility to enjoy anything—even pride.

But what we suffer from today is humility in the wrong place. Modesty has moved from the organ of ambition. Modesty has settled upon the organ of conviction; where it was never meant to be. A man was meant to be doubtful about himself, but undoubting about the truth; this has been exactly reversed. Nowadays the part of a man that a man does assert is exactly the part he ought not to assert—himself. The part he doubts is exactly the part he ought not to doubt—the Divine Reason. Huxley preached a humility content to learn from Nature.[5] But the new sceptic is so humble that he doubts if he can even learn.

Thus we should be wrong if we had said hastily that there is no humility typical of our time. The truth is that there is a real humility

---

[5] Thomas Henry Huxley (1825–95) was an English biologist, known as "Darwin's Bulldog" for his strong advocacy of Charles Darwin's theory of evolution.

typical of our time; but it so happens that it is practically a more poisonous humility than the wildest prostrations of the ascetic. The old humility was a spur that prevented a man from stopping; not a nail in his boot that prevented him from going on. For the old humility made a man doubtful about his efforts, which might make him work harder. But the new humility makes a man doubtful about his aims, which will make him stop working altogether.

At any street corner we may meet a man who utters the frantic and blasphemous statement that he may be wrong. Every day one comes across somebody who says that of course his view may not be the right one. Of course his view must be the right one, or it is not his view. We are on the road to producing a race of men too mentally modest to believe in the multiplication table. We are in danger of seeing philosophers who doubt the law of gravity as being a mere fancy of their own. Scoffers of old time were too proud to be convinced; but these are too humble to be convinced. The meek do inherit the earth;[6] but the modern sceptics are too meek even to claim their inheritance. It is exactly this intellectual helplessness which is our second problem.

The Peril of Intellectual Self-Destruction

The last chapter has been concerned only with a fact of observation: that what peril of morbidity there is for man comes rather from his reason than his imagination. It was not meant to attack the authority of reason; rather it is the ultimate purpose to defend it. For it needs defence. The whole modern world is at war with reason; and the tower already reels.

The sages, it is often said, can see no answer to the riddle of religion. But the trouble with our sages is not that they cannot see the answer; it is that they cannot even see the riddle. They are like children so stupid as to notice nothing paradoxical in the playful

[6] From Jesus's Sermon on the Mount (Matt 5:5).

assertion that a door is not a door. The modern latitudinarians speak,[7] for instance, about authority in religion not only as if there were no reason in it, but as if there had never been any reason for it. Apart from seeing its philosophical basis, they cannot even see its historical cause. Religious authority has often, doubtless, been oppressive or unreasonable; just as every legal system (and especially our present one) has been callous and full of a cruel apathy. It is rational to attack the police; nay, it is glorious. But the modern critics of religious authority are like men who should attack the police without ever having heard of burglars. For there is a great and possible peril to the human mind: a peril as practical as burglary. Against it religious authority was reared, rightly or wrongly, as a barrier. And against it something certainly must be reared as a barrier, if our race is to avoid ruin.

That peril is that the human intellect is free to destroy itself. Just as one generation could prevent the very existence of the next generation, by all entering a monastery or jumping into the sea, so one set of thinkers can in some degree prevent further thinking by teaching the next generation that there is no validity in any human thought.

It is idle to talk always of the alternative of reason and faith. Reason is itself a matter of faith. It is an act of faith to assert that our thoughts have any relation to reality at all. If you are merely a sceptic, you must sooner or later ask yourself the question, "Why should *anything* go right; even observation and deduction? Why should not good logic be as misleading as bad logic? They are both movements in the brain of a bewildered ape?"

The young sceptic says, "I have a right to think for myself."

---

[7] The latitudinarians were a group of seventeenth-century English theologians known for moderation in controversies over specific doctrines or religious practices. Chesterton refers to "modern latitudinarians" as those who believe the differences between varying creeds or forms of worship are unimportant.

But the old sceptic, the complete sceptic, says, "I have no right to think for myself. I have no right to think at all."

There is a thought that stops thought. That is the only thought that ought to be stopped. That is the ultimate evil against which all religious authority was aimed. It only appears at the end of decadent ages like our own: and already Mr. H. G. Wells has raised its ruinous banner; he has written a delicate piece of scepticism called "Doubts of the Instrument."[8] In this he questions the brain itself, and endeavours to remove all reality from all his own assertions, past, present, and to come.

But it was against this remote ruin that all the military systems in religion were originally ranked and ruled. The creeds and the crusades, the hierarchies and the horrible persecutions were not organized, as is ignorantly said, for the suppression of reason. They were organized for the difficult defence of reason. Man, by a blind instinct, knew that if once things were wildly questioned, reason could be questioned first. The authority of priests to absolve, the authority of popes to define the authority, even of inquisitors to terrify: these were all only dark defences erected round one central authority, more undemonstrable, more supernatural than all—the authority of a man to think.

We know now that this is so; we have no excuse for not knowing it. For we can hear scepticism crashing through the old ring of authorities, and at the same moment we can see reason swaying upon her throne. Insofar as religion is gone, reason is going. For they are both of the same primary and authoritative kind. They are both methods of proof which cannot themselves be proved. And in the act of destroying the idea of Divine authority, we have largely destroyed the idea of that human authority by which we

---

[8] H. G. Wells (1866–1946) was an English writer of many genres, best known today for his science fiction novels, including *The Invisible Man* and *The War of the Worlds.* Chesterton is referring to a paper—"Scepticism of the Instrument"—that Wells read before the Oxford Philosophical Society in 1903.

do a long-division sum. With a long and sustained tug we have attempted to pull the mitre off pontifical man; and his head has come off with it.

Modern Fashions That Stop Thought

Lest this should be called loose assertion, it is perhaps desirable, though dull, to run rapidly through the chief modern fashions of thought which have this effect of stopping thought itself.

Materialism and the World as Unreal

Materialism and the view of everything as a personal illusion have some such effect; for if the mind is mechanical, thought cannot be very exciting, and if the cosmos is unreal, there is nothing to think about. But in these cases the effect is indirect and doubtful. In some cases it is direct and clear; notably in the case of what is generally called evolution.

Evolution

Evolution is a good example of that modern intelligence which, if it destroys anything, destroys itself. Evolution is either an innocent scientific description of how certain earthly things came about; or, if it is anything more than this, it is an attack upon thought itself. If evolution destroys anything, it does not destroy religion but rationalism. If evolution simply means that a positive thing called an ape turned very slowly into a positive thing called a man, then it is stingless for the most orthodox; for a personal God might just as well do things slowly as quickly, especially if, like the Christian God, he were outside time. But if it means anything more, it means that there is no such thing as an ape to change, and no such thing as a man for him to change into. It means that there is no such thing as a thing. At best, there is only one thing, and that is a flux of everything and anything.

This is an attack not upon the faith, but upon the mind; you cannot think if there are no things to think about. You cannot think if you are not separate from the subject of thought.

Descartes said, "I think; therefore I am."[9]

The philosophic evolutionist reverses and negatives the epigram. He says, "I am not; therefore I cannot think."

Rationalism / "Free Thought"

Then there is the opposite attack on thought: that urged by Mr. H. G. Wells when he insists that every separate thing is "unique," and there are no categories at all. This also is merely destructive. Thinking means connecting things, and stops if they cannot be connected. It need hardly be said that this scepticism forbidding thought necessarily forbids speech; a man cannot open his mouth without contradicting it. Thus when Mr. Wells says (as he did somewhere), "All chairs are quite different," he utters not merely a misstatement, but a contradiction in terms. If all chairs were quite different, you could not call them "all chairs."

The False Theory of Progress

Akin to these is the false theory of progress, which maintains that we alter the test instead of trying to pass the test.

We often hear it said, for instance, "What is right in one age is wrong in another." This is quite reasonable, if it means that there is a fixed aim, and that certain methods attain at certain times and not at other times. If women, say, desire to be elegant, it may be that they are improved at one time by growing fatter and at another time by growing thinner. But you cannot say that they are improved by ceasing to wish to be elegant and beginning to wish to be oblong.

---

[9] René Descartes (1596–1650) was a French philosopher, mathematician, and scientist, widely regarded as one of the founders of modern philosophy.

If the standard changes, how can there be improvement, which implies a standard?

Nietzsche started a nonsensical idea that men had once sought as good what we now call evil;[10] if it were so, we could not talk of surpassing or even falling short of them. How can you overtake Jones if you walk in the other direction? You cannot discuss whether one people has succeeded more in being miserable than another succeeded in being happy. It would be like discussing whether Milton was more puritanical than a pig is fat.[11]

It is true that a man (a silly man) might make change itself his object or ideal. But as an ideal, change itself becomes unchangeable. If the change-worshipper wishes to estimate his own progress, he must be sternly loyal to the ideal of change; he must not begin to flirt gaily with the ideal of monotony. Progress itself cannot progress. It is worth remark, in passing, that when Tennyson, in a wild and rather weak manner, welcomed the idea of infinite alteration in society, he instinctively took a metaphor which suggests an imprisoned tedium. He wrote—

Let the great world spin for ever down the ringing grooves of change.[12]

He thought of change itself as an unchangeable groove; and so it is. Change is about the narrowest and hardest groove that a man can get into.

The main point here, however, is that this idea of a fundamental alteration in the standard is one of the things that make thought about the past or future simply impossible. The theory of a complete change of standards in human history does not merely deprive us

---

[10] Friedrich Nietzsche (1844–1900) was a German philosopher known for his rejection of traditional morality and his belief that God was a creation of man rather than the other way around.

[11] John Milton (1608–74) was the great Puritan poet best known for his epic *Paradise Lost*, now considered one of the world's greatest works of literature.

[12] A line from Alfred Lord Tennyson (1809–92), who remains one of Britain's most beloved poets.

of the pleasure of honouring our fathers; it deprives us even of the more modern and aristocratic pleasure of despising them.

Pragmatism

This bald summary of the thought-destroying forces of our time would not be complete without some reference to pragmatism; for though I have here used and should everywhere defend the pragmatist method as a preliminary guide to truth, there is an extreme application of it which involves the absence of all truth whatever.

My meaning can be put shortly thus. I agree with the pragmatists that apparent objective truth is not the whole matter; that there is an authoritative need to believe the things that are necessary to the human mind. But I say that one of those necessities precisely is a belief in objective truth.

The pragmatist tells a man to think what he must think and never mind the Absolute. But precisely one of the things that he must think is the Absolute. This philosophy, indeed, is a kind of verbal paradox. Pragmatism is a matter of human needs; and one of the first of human needs is to be something more than a pragmatist. Extreme pragmatism is just as inhuman as the determinism it so powerfully attacks. The determinist (who, to do him justice, does not pretend to be a human being) makes nonsense of the human sense of actual choice. The pragmatist, who professes to be specially human, makes nonsense of the human sense of actual fact.

The Suicidal Mania of Modern Philosophies

To sum up our contention so far, we may say that the most characteristic current philosophies have not only a touch of mania, but a touch of suicidal mania. The mere questioner has knocked his head against the limits of human thought; and cracked it. This is what makes so futile the warnings of the orthodox and the boasts of the advanced about the dangerous boyhood of free thought. What we are looking at is not the boyhood of free thought; it is the old age and ultimate dissolution of free thought.

It is vain for bishops and pious bigwigs to discuss what dreadful things will happen if wild scepticism runs its course. It has run its course.

It is vain for eloquent atheists to talk of the great truths that will be revealed if once we see free thought begin. We have seen it end. It has no more questions to ask; it has questioned itself.

You cannot call up any wilder vision than a city in which men ask themselves if they have any selves. You cannot fancy a more sceptical world than that in which men doubt if there is a world.

It might certainly have reached its bankruptcy more quickly and cleanly if it had not been feebly hampered by the application of indefensible laws of blasphemy or by the absurd pretence that modern England is Christian. But it would have reached the bankruptcy anyhow. Militant atheists are still unjustly persecuted; but rather because they are an old minority than because they are a new one. Free thought has exhausted its own freedom. It is weary of its own success. If any eager freethinker now hails philosophic freedom as the dawn, he is only like the man in Mark Twain who came out wrapped in blankets to see the sun rise and was just in time to see it set.[13] If any frightened curate still says that it will be awful if the darkness of free thought should spread, we can only answer him in the high and powerful words of Mr. Belloc,[14] "Do not, I beseech you, be troubled about the increase of forces already in dissolution. You have mistaken the hour of the night: it is already morning." We have no more questions left to ask. We have looked for questions in the darkest corners and on the wildest peaks. We have found all the questions that can be found. It is time we gave up looking for questions and began looking for answers.

---

[13] A memorable moment from Mark Twain's novel *A Tramp Abroad,* published in 1880.

[14] Hilaire Belloc (1870–1953) was a prolific writer and one of Chesterton's closest friends and frequent collaborators.

But one more word must be added. At the beginning of this preliminary negative sketch I said that our mental ruin has been wrought by wild reason, not by wild imagination. A man does not go mad because he makes a statue a mile high, but he may go mad by thinking it out in square inches.

The Worship of the Will

Now, one school of thinkers has seen this and jumped at it as a way of renewing the pagan health of the world. They see that reason destroys; but Will, they say, creates. The ultimate authority, they say, is in will, not in reason. The supreme point is not why a man demands a thing, but the fact that he does demand it.

I have no space to trace or expound this philosophy of Will. It came, I suppose, through Nietzsche, who preached something that is called egoism. That, indeed, was simpleminded enough; for Nietzsche denied egoism simply by preaching it. To preach anything is to give it away. First, the egoist calls life a war without mercy, and then he takes the greatest possible trouble to drill his enemies in war. To preach egoism is to practise altruism. But however it began, the view is common enough in current literature.

The main defence of these thinkers is that they are not thinkers; they are makers. They say that choice is itself the divine thing. Thus Mr. Bernard Shaw has attacked the old idea that men's acts are to be judged by the standard of the desire of happiness. He says that a man does not act for his happiness, but from his will. He does not say, "Jam will make me happy," but "I want jam."

And in all this others follow him with yet greater enthusiasm. Mr. John Davidson, a remarkable poet,[15] is so passionately excited about it that he is obliged to write prose. He publishes a short play with several long prefaces. This is natural enough in Mr. Shaw, for all his plays are prefaces: Mr. Shaw is (I suspect) the only man on

---

[15] John Davidson (1857–1909) was a Scottish playwright and novelist, best known for his ballads.

earth who has never written any poetry. But that Mr. Davidson (who can write excellent poetry) should write instead laborious metaphysics in defence of this doctrine of will, does show that the doctrine of will has taken hold of men.

Even Mr. H. G. Wells has half spoken in its language; saying that one should test acts not like a thinker, but like an artist, saying, "I *feel* this curve is right," or "that line *shall* go thus." They are all excited; and well they may be. For by this doctrine of the divine authority of will, they think they can break out of the doomed fortress of rationalism. They think they can escape.

But they cannot escape. This pure praise of volition ends in the same break up and blank as the mere pursuit of logic. Exactly as complete free thought involves the doubting of thought itself, so the acceptation of mere "willing" really paralyzes the will. Mr. Bernard Shaw has not perceived the real difference between the old utilitarian test of pleasure (clumsy, of course, and easily misstated) and that which he propounds.[16] The real difference between the test of happiness and the test of will is simply that the test of happiness is a test and the other isn't.

You can discuss whether a man's act in jumping over a cliff was directed towards happiness; you cannot discuss whether it was derived from will. Of course it was.

You can praise an action by saying that it is calculated to bring pleasure or pain to discover truth or to save the soul. But you cannot praise an action because it shows will; for to say that is merely to say that it is an action.

By this praise of will you cannot really choose one course as better than another. And yet choosing one course as better than another is the very definition of the will you are praising.

The worship of will is the negation of will. To admire mere choice is to refuse to choose.

---

[16] Here, Chesterton is referring to the philosophical claim that pleasure, or the principle of greatest happiness, must be the measure of right and wrong. Jeremy Bentham (1748–1832) was a proponent of this perspective.

If Mr. Bernard Shaw comes up to me and says, "Will something," that is tantamount to saying, "I do not mind what you will," and that is tantamount to saying, "I have no will in the matter." You cannot admire will in general, because the essence of will is that it is particular.

A brilliant anarchist like Mr. John Davidson feels an irritation against ordinary morality, and therefore he invokes will—will to anything. He only wants humanity to want something. But humanity does want something. It wants ordinary morality. He rebels against the law and tells us to will something or anything. But we have willed something. We have willed the law against which he rebels.

The Will in the World of Limits

All the will-worshippers, from Nietzsche to Mr. Davidson, are really quite empty of volition. They cannot will, they can hardly wish. And if any one wants a proof of this, it can be found quite easily. It can be found in this fact: that they always talk of will as something that expands and breaks out. But it is quite the opposite. Every act of will is an act of self-limitation. To desire action is to desire limitation. In that sense every act is an act of self-sacrifice. When you choose anything, you reject everything else.

That objection, which men of this school used to make to the act of marriage, is really an objection to every act. Every act is an irrevocable selection and exclusion. Just as when you marry one woman you give up all the others, so when you take one course of action you give up all the other courses. If you become King of England, you give up the post of Beadle in Brompton.[17] If you go to Rome, you sacrifice a rich suggestive life in Wimbledon. It is the existence of this negative or limiting side of will that makes most of the talk of the anarchic will-worshippers little better than nonsense.

---

[17] A beadle is a minor official who carries out various civil, educational, or ceremonial duties on an English manor.

For instance, Mr. John Davidson tells us to have nothing to do with "Thou shalt not"; but it is surely obvious that "Thou shalt not" is only one of the necessary corollaries of "I will." "I will go to the Lord Mayor's Show, and thou shalt not stop me."

Anarchism adjures us to be bold creative artists, and care for no laws or limits. But it is impossible to be an artist and not care for laws and limits. Art is limitation; the essence of every picture is the frame.

If you draw a giraffe, you must draw him with a long neck. If, in your bold creative way, you hold yourself free to draw a giraffe with a short neck, you will really find that you are not free to draw a giraffe. The moment you step into the world of facts, you step into a world of limits. You can free things from alien or accidental laws, but not from the laws of their own nature. You may, if you like, free a tiger from his bars; but do not free him from his stripes. Do not free a camel of the burden of his hump: you may be freeing him from being a camel. Do not go about as a demagogue, encouraging triangles to break out of the prison of their three sides. If a triangle breaks out of its three sides, its life comes to a lamentable end. Somebody wrote a work called "The Loves of the Triangles"; I never read it, but I am sure that if triangles ever were loved, they were loved for being triangular.

This is certainly the case with all artistic creation, which is in some ways the most decisive example of pure will. The artist loves his limitations: they constitute the *thing* he is doing. The painter is glad that the canvas is flat. The sculptor is glad that the clay is colourless.

The Doubts of the Modern Man in Revolt

In case the point is not clear, an historic example may illustrate it. The French Revolution was really an heroic and decisive thing, because the Jacobins willed something definite and limited.[18] They

[18] The Jacobins were the most influential political force during the French Revolution of 1789.

desired the freedoms of democracy, but also all the vetoes of democracy. They wished to have votes and *not* to have titles. Republicanism had an ascetic side in Franklin or Robespierre as well as an expansive side in Danton or Wilkes.[19] Therefore they have created something with a solid substance and shape, the square social equality and peasant wealth of France.

But since then the revolutionary or speculative mind of Europe has been weakened by shrinking from any proposal because of the limits of that proposal. Liberalism has been degraded into liberality. Men have tried to turn "revolutionise" from a transitive to an intransitive verb.

The Jacobin could tell you not only the system he would rebel against, but (what was more important) the system he would *not* rebel against, the system he would trust. But the new rebel is a Sceptic, and will not entirely trust anything. He has no loyalty; therefore he can never be really a revolutionist. And the fact that he doubts everything really gets in his way when he wants to denounce anything. For all denunciation implies a moral doctrine of some kind; and the modern revolutionist doubts not only the institution he denounces, but the doctrine by which he denounces it.

Thus he writes one book complaining that imperial oppression insults the purity of women, and then he writes another book (about the sex problem) in which he insults it himself.

He curses the Sultan because Christian girls lose their virginity, and then curses Mrs. Grundy because they keep it.[20]

As a politician, he will cry out that war is a waste of life, and then, as a philosopher, that all life is waste of time.

---

[19] Ben Franklin (1706–90) was one of America's founders; Maximilien Robespierre (1758–94) was one of the most influential figures of the French Revolution. Georges Danton (1759–94) was a leading figure in the early stage of the French Revolution; John Wilkes (1725–97) was a British champion of the rights of the individual.

[20] Mrs. Grundy is a general name for someone extremely conventional or priggish, a personification of being obsessed with personal purity.

A Russian pessimist will denounce a policeman for killing a peasant, and then prove by the highest philosophical principles that the peasant ought to have killed himself.

A man denounces marriage as a lie, and then denounces aristocratic profligates for treating it as a lie.

He calls a flag a bauble, and then blames the oppressors of Poland or Ireland because they take away that bauble.

The man of this school goes first to a political meeting, where he complains that savages are treated as if they were beasts; then he takes his hat and umbrella and goes on to a scientific meeting, where he proves that they practically are beasts.

In short, the modern revolutionist, being an infinite sceptic, is always engaged in undermining his own mines. In his book on politics he attacks men for trampling on morality; in his book on ethics he attacks morality for trampling on men. Therefore the modern man in revolt has become practically useless for all purposes of revolt. By rebelling against everything he has lost his right to rebel against anything.

Satire without a Standard

It may be added that the same blank and bankruptcy can be observed in all fierce and terrible types of literature, especially in satire. Satire may be mad and anarchic, but it presupposes an admitted superiority in certain things over others; it presupposes a standard. When little boys in the street laugh at the fatness of some distinguished journalist, they are unconsciously assuming a standard of Greek sculpture. They are appealing to the marble Apollo. And the curious disappearance of satire from our literature is an instance of the fierce things fading for want of any principle to be fierce about.

Nietzsche had some natural talent for sarcasm: he could sneer, though he could not laugh; but there is always something bodiless and without weight in his satire, simply because it has not any mass of common morality behind it. He is himself more preposterous than anything he denounces.

But, indeed, Nietzsche will stand very well as the type of the whole of this failure of abstract violence. The softening of the brain which ultimately overtook him was not a physical accident. If Nietzsche had not ended in imbecility, Nietzscheism would end in imbecility. Thinking in isolation and with pride ends in being an idiot. Every man who will not have softening of the heart must at last have softening of the brain.

This last attempt to evade intellectualism ends in intellectualism, and therefore in death. The sortie has failed. The wild worship of lawlessness and the materialist worship of law end in the same void. Nietzsche scales staggering mountains, but he turns up ultimately in Tibet. He sits down beside Tolstoy in the land of nothing and Nirvana.[21] They are both helpless—one because he must not grasp anything, and the other because he must not let go of anything. The Tolstoyan's will is frozen by a Buddhist instinct that all special actions are evil. But the Nietzscheite's will is quite equally frozen by his view that all special actions are good; for if all special actions are good, none of them are special. They stand at the cross-roads, and one hates all the roads and the other likes all the roads. The result is—well, some things are not hard to calculate. They stand at the cross-roads.

Joan of Arc and Jesus vs. Nietzsche, Tolstoy, and the Philosophers

Here I end (thank God) the first and dullest business of this book—the rough review of recent thought. After this I begin to sketch a view of life which may not interest my reader, but which, at any rate, interests me.

In front of me, as I close this page, is a pile of modern books that I have been turning over for the purpose—a pile of ingenuity, a pile of futility. By the accident of my present detachment, I

[21] Leo Tolstoy (1828–1910), the famous Russian writer known for his austere moral views.

can see the inevitable smash of the philosophies of Schopenhauer and Tolstoy,[22] Nietzsche and Shaw, as clearly as an inevitable railway smash could be seen from a balloon. They are all on the road to the emptiness of the asylum. For madness may be defined as using mental activity so as to reach mental helplessness; and they have nearly reached it. He who thinks he is made of glass, thinks to the destruction of thought; for glass cannot think. So he who wills to reject nothing, wills the destruction of will; for will is not only the choice of something, but the rejection of almost everything.

And as I turn and tumble over the clever, wonderful, tiresome, and useless modern books, the title of one of them rivets my eye. It is called *Jeanne d'Arc*, by Anatole France.[23] I have only glanced at it, but a glance was enough to remind me of Renan's *Vie de Jesus*.[24] It has the same strange method of the reverent sceptic. It discredits supernatural stories that have some foundation, simply by telling natural stories that have no foundation. Because we cannot believe in what a saint did, we are to pretend that we know exactly what he felt. But I do not mention either book in order to criticise it, but because the accidental combination of the names called up two startling images of Sanity which blasted all the books before me.

Joan of Arc was not stuck at the cross-roads, either by rejecting all the paths like Tolstoy, or by accepting them all like Nietzsche. She chose a path, and went down it like a thunderbolt. Yet Joan, when I came to think of her, had in her all that was true either in Tolstoy or Nietzsche, all that was even tolerable in either of them. I

---

[22] Arthur Schopenhauer (1788–1860) was a German philosopher best known for his work characterizing the world as the product of a blind and insatiable metaphysical will.

[23] "Anatole France" was the pseudonym for Jacques Anatole Thibault, who wrote a biography of Joan of Arc in 1908 that portrayed her as suffering under hallucination and as submitting to the powerful pull of the clergy of her day.

[24] Joseph Ernest Renan (1823–92) was a French writer, best known for his popular 1863 book *The Life of Jesus*, to which Chesterton refers here. Renan portrayed Christ as an inspired but merely human teacher.

thought of all that is noble in Tolstoy, the pleasure in plain things, especially in plain pity, the actualities of the earth, the reverence for the poor, the dignity of the bowed back. Joan of Arc had all that and with this great addition, that she endured poverty as well as admiring it; whereas Tolstoy is only a typical aristocrat trying to find out its secret.

And then I thought of all that was brave and proud and pathetic in poor Nietzsche, and his mutiny against the emptiness and timidity of our time. I thought of his cry for the ecstatic equilibrium of danger, his hunger for the rush of great horses, his cry to arms. Well, Joan of Arc had all that, and again with this difference, that she did not praise fighting, but fought. We *know* that she was not afraid of an army, while Nietzsche, for all we know, was afraid of a cow. Tolstoy only praised the peasant; she was the peasant. Nietzsche only praised the warrior; she was the warrior. She beat them both at their own antagonistic ideals; she was more gentle than the one, more violent than the other. Yet she was a perfectly practical person who did something, while they are wild speculators who do nothing. It was impossible that the thought should not cross my mind that she and her faith had perhaps some secret of moral unity and utility that has been lost.

And with that thought came a larger one, and the colossal figure of her Master had also crossed the theatre of my thoughts. The same modern difficulty which darkened the subject-matter of Anatole France also darkened that of Ernest Renan. Renan also divided his hero's pity from his hero's pugnacity. Renan even represented the righteous anger at Jerusalem as a mere nervous breakdown after the idyllic expectations of Galilee. As if there were any inconsistency between having a love for humanity and having a hatred for inhumanity! Altruists, with thin, weak voices, denounce Christ as an egoist. Egoists (with even thinner and weaker voices) denounce Him as an altruist. In our present atmosphere such cavils are comprehensible enough. The love of a hero is more terrible than the hatred of a tyrant. The hatred of a hero is more generous than the love of a philanthropist.

There is a huge and heroic sanity of which moderns can only collect the fragments. There is a giant of whom we see only the lopped arms and legs walking about. They have torn the soul of Christ into silly strips, labelled egoism and altruism, and they are equally puzzled by His insane magnificence and His insane meekness. They have parted His garments among them, and for His vesture they have cast lots;[25] though the coat was without seam woven from the top throughout.

[25] In the Gospel accounts of Christ's crucifixion, the soldiers at the cross rend Jesus's garments and cast lots for his clothing (Matt 27:35).

Chapter Summary

In this chapter Chesterton completed his survey of philosophies popular in his time, in order to show that all of them lead to a dead end due to their contradictions. He began by explaining how bits and pieces of Christianity (namely, Christian virtues) have been cut loose from the whole of Christianity, with damaging effects on the world. Humility is an example—modesty should mark a person's ambition, not their conviction. Chesterton surveyed several philosophical streams—including scepticism, materialism, evolution, and pragmatism—in order to show how each of these patterns of thought result in the stopping of further thought. They set themselves over against religious authority, in defense of reason. But Chesterton claimed that it is religious authority (and the recognition that any first principle must be taken by faith) that makes room for reason.

A possible way out of this conundrum seems to lie in some philosophers' turn to the exaltation of the Will over reason, following in the path of Nietzsche. But, as Chesterton explained, those who elevate the Will in this way cannot do so generally. We live in a world of limits, and acts of will are inherently limiting. He closed the chapter with the example of Joan of Arc in contrast to Nietzsche, a foreshadowing of a theme he will address more fully in chapter 6—the importance of paradox.

Discussion Questions

1. What do you think about Chesterton's claim that the Christian virtues, when detached from each other, do more harm in the world than people's vices?
2. Chesterton claims that the notion of progress makes no sense apart from having some sort of standard or ideal. How should we think about this standard? Where does it come from?

3. As Chesterton points out, every act of the will is an act of self-limitation. Every time you choose something, you are *not* choosing something else. What implications does this truth have for a culture that believes freedom lies in having unending choices?

FOUR

"The Ethics of Elfland" is one of the most well-known chapters in *Orthodoxy*. Although a couple others are strong contenders for me, I keep coming back to this one as my favorite. Here, Chesterton begins to construct an ethical system grounded in childlike wonder and a deep and abiding sense of gratitude. How does he do this? By returning to the fairy tales of his youth and recapturing something of the magic of this world in which we find ourselves. The world is as strange and wondrous as any fairy tale we've been told, and if it has any meaning at all, there must be someone to mean it—a Storyteller behind it all.

Chesterton's goal in this chapter is to continue the argument he began in the previous chapters; here he claims that the world is not logically necessary. This is the first principle that we must accept. We must accept the world as a gift, not try to rationalize it or explain it away or question everything about it (attempts we saw in chapters 2 and 3). How do we receive this gift? By opening our eyes and seeing the world with childlike astonishment, and then by recapturing that real wonder at the real world over and over again.

Memorable Parts to Look For

- The democracy of the dead
- Urging thanksgiving for the birthday present of birth

- Repetition in nature comes from God saying, "Do it again!"
- The fairy godmother philosophy
- The *Robinson Crusoe* illustration

The Ethics of Elfland

When the business man rebukes the idealism of his office-boy, it is commonly in some such speech as this: "Ah, yes, when one is young, one has these ideals in the abstract and these castles in the air; but in middle age they all break up like clouds, and one comes down to a belief in practical politics, to using the machinery one has and getting on with the world as it is." Thus, at least, venerable and philanthropic old men now in their honoured graves used to talk to me when I was a boy.

But since then I have grown up and have discovered that these philanthropic old men were telling lies. What has really happened is exactly the opposite of what they said would happen. They said that I should lose my ideals and begin to believe in the methods of practical politicians. Now, I have not lost my ideals in the least; my faith in fundamentals is exactly what it always was. What I have lost is my old childlike faith in practical politics. I am still as much concerned as ever about the Battle of Armageddon;[1] but I am not so much concerned about the General Election. As a babe I leapt up on my mother's knee at the mere mention of it. No; the vision is

[1] The epic battle between good and evil as described in Revelation, the last book of the Bible.

always solid and reliable. The vision is always a fact. It is the reality that is often a fraud. As much as I ever did, more than I ever did, I believe in Liberalism. But there was a rosy time of innocence when I believed in Liberals.

Democracy in Two Propositions

I take this instance of one of the enduring faiths because, having now to trace the roots of my personal speculation, this may be counted, I think, as the only positive bias. I was brought up a Liberal, and have always believed in democracy, in the elementary liberal doctrine of a self-governing humanity. If any one finds the phrase vague or threadbare, I can only pause for a moment to explain that the principle of democracy, as I mean it, can be stated in two propositions.

The first is this: that the things common to all men are more important than the things peculiar to any men. Ordinary things are more valuable than extraordinary things; nay, they are more extraordinary. Man is something more awful than men; something more strange. The sense of the miracle of humanity itself should be always more vivid to us than any marvels of power, intellect, art, or civilization. The mere man on two legs, as such, should be felt as something more heartbreaking than any music and more startling than any caricature. Death is more tragic even than death by starvation. Having a nose is more comic even than having a Norman nose.[2]

This is the first principle of democracy: that the essential things in men are the things they hold in common, not the things they hold separately. And the second principle is merely this: that the political instinct or desire is one of these things which they hold in common.

Falling in love is more poetical than dropping into poetry. The democratic contention is that government (helping to rule the

[2] A nose with a prominent bridge, now known as aqualine.

tribe) is a thing like falling in love, and not a thing like dropping into poetry. It is not something analogous to playing the church organ, painting on vellum, discovering the North Pole (that insidious habit), looping the loop, being Astronomer Royal, and so on. For these things we do not wish a man to do at all unless he does them well. It is, on the contrary, a thing analogous to writing one's own love-letters or blowing one's own nose. These things we want a man to do for himself, even if he does them badly.

I am not here arguing the truth of any of these conceptions; I know that some moderns are asking to have their wives chosen by scientists, and they may soon be asking, for all I know, to have their noses blown by nurses. I merely say that mankind does recognize these universal human functions, and that democracy classes government among them. In short, the democratic faith is this: that the most terribly important things must be left to ordinary men themselves—the mating of the sexes, the rearing of the young, the laws of the state. This is democracy; and in this I have always believed.

The Democracy of the Dead

But there is one thing that I have never from my youth up been able to understand. I have never been able to understand where people got the idea that democracy was in some way opposed to tradition. It is obvious that tradition is only democracy extended through time. It is trusting to a consensus of common human voices rather than to some isolated or arbitrary record.

The man who quotes some German historian against the tradition of the Catholic Church, for instance, is strictly appealing to aristocracy. He is appealing to the superiority of one expert against the awful authority of a mob. It is quite easy to see why a legend is treated, and ought to be treated, more respectfully than a book of history. The legend is generally made by the majority of people in the village, who are sane. The book is generally written by the one man in the village who is mad.

Those who urge against tradition that men in the past were ignorant may go and urge it at the Carlton Club,[3] along with the statement that voters in the slums are ignorant. It will not do for us. If we attach great importance to the opinion of ordinary men in great unanimity when we are dealing with daily matters, there is no reason why we should disregard it when we are dealing with history or fable.

Tradition may be defined as an extension of the franchise. Tradition means giving votes to the most obscure of all classes, our ancestors. It is the democracy of the dead. Tradition refuses to submit to the small and arrogant oligarchy of those who merely happen to be walking about. All democrats object to men being disqualified by the accident of birth; tradition objects to their being disqualified by the accident of death. Democracy tells us not to neglect a good man's opinion, even if he is our groom;[4] tradition asks us not to neglect a good man's opinion, even if he is our father.

I, at any rate, cannot separate the two ideas of democracy and tradition; it seems evident to me that they are the same idea. We will have the dead at our councils. The ancient Greeks voted by stones; these shall vote by tombstones. It is all quite regular and official, for most tombstones, like most ballot papers, are marked with a cross.

I have first to say, therefore, that if I have had a bias, it was always a bias in favour of democracy, and therefore of tradition. Before we come to any theoretic or logical beginnings I am content to allow for that personal equation; I have always been more inclined to believe the ruck of hard-working people than to believe that special and troublesome literary class to which I belong. I prefer even the fancies and prejudices of the people who see life from the inside to the clearest demonstrations of the people who see life from the outside.

---

[3] One of London's foremost "members-only" clubs, founded in 1832.

[4] "Groom" here refers not to a man on his wedding day, but to the man whose job was to take care of another's horse.

I would always trust the old wives' fables against the old maids' facts. As long as wit is mother wit it can be as wild as it pleases.

The Fundamental Tenets of My Personal Philosophy

Now, I have to put together a general position, and I pretend to no training in such things. I propose to do it, therefore, by writing down one after another the three or four fundamental ideas which I have found for myself, pretty much in the way that I found them. Then I shall roughly synthesise them, summing up my personal philosophy or natural religion; then I shall describe my startling discovery that the whole thing had been discovered before. It had been discovered by Christianity.

But of these profound persuasions which I have to recount in order, the earliest was concerned with this element of popular tradition. And without the foregoing explanation touching tradition and democracy I could hardly make my mental experience clear. As it is, I do not know whether I can make it clear, but I now propose to try.

Truth in Tales from the Nursery

My first and last philosophy, that which I believe in with unbroken certainty, I learnt in the nursery. I generally learnt it from a nurse; that is, from the solemn and star-appointed priestess at once of democracy and tradition.

The things I believed most then, the things I believe most now, are the things called fairy tales. They seem to me to be the entirely reasonable things. They are not fantasies: compared with them other things are fantastic. Compared with them religion and rationalism are both abnormal, though religion is abnormally right and rationalism abnormally wrong. Fairyland is nothing but the sunny country of common sense. It is not earth that judges heaven, but heaven that judges earth; so for me at least it was not earth that criticised elfland, but elfland that criticised the earth. I knew the magic beanstalk before I had tasted beans; I was sure of the Man in the Moon before I was certain of the moon.

This was at one with all popular tradition. Modern minor poets are naturalists, and talk about the bush or the brook; but the singers of the old epics and fables were supernaturalists, and talked about the gods of brook and bush. That is what the moderns mean when they say that the ancients did not "appreciate Nature," because they said that Nature was divine. Old nurses do not tell children about the grass, but about the fairies that dance on the grass; and the old Greeks could not see the trees for the dryads.

But I deal here with what ethic and philosophy come from being fed on fairy tales. If I were describing them in detail I could note many noble and healthy principles that arise from them.

There is the chivalrous lesson of "Jack the Giant Killer"; that giants should be killed because they are gigantic. It is a manly mutiny against pride as such. For the rebel is older than all the kingdoms, and the Jacobin has more tradition than the Jacobite.[5]

There is the lesson of "Cinderella," which is the same as that of the Magnificat—*exaltavit humiles.*[6]

There is the great lesson of "Beauty and the Beast"; that a thing must be loved *before* it is loveable.

There is the terrible allegory of the "Sleeping Beauty," which tells how the human creature was blessed with all birthday gifts, yet cursed with death; and how death also may perhaps be softened to a sleep.

---

[5] The Jacobin was a member of a political group that overthrew the king in the French Revolution. The Jacobite was a Scottish supporter of the House of Stuart after the Revolution of 1688, when James II (the last Stuart king) was deposed.

[6] The Magnificat is Mary's prayer upon being told she would be the mother of Jesus (Luke 1:46–55). *Exaltavit humiles* is Latin for the phrase "exalted the humble" (v. 52).

The Laws of Elfland

But I am not concerned with any of the separate statutes of elfland, but with the whole spirit of its law, which I learnt before I could speak, and shall retain when I cannot write. I am concerned with a certain way of looking at life, which was created in me by the fairy tales, but has since been meekly ratified by the mere facts.

It might be stated this way. There are certain sequences or developments (cases of one thing following another), which are, in the true sense of the word, reasonable. They are, in the true sense of the word, necessary. Such are mathematical and merely logical sequences. We in fairyland (who are the most reasonable of all creatures) admit that reason and that necessity.

For instance, if the Ugly Sisters are older than Cinderella, it is (in an iron and awful sense) *necessary* that Cinderella is younger than the Ugly Sisters. There is no getting out of it. Haeckel may talk as much fatalism about that fact as he pleases: it really must be. If Jack is the son of a miller, a miller is the father of Jack. Cold reason decrees it from her awful throne: and we in fairyland submit. If the three brothers all ride horses, there are six animals and eighteen legs involved: that is true rationalism, and fairyland is full of it.

But as I put my head over the hedge of the elves and began to take notice of the natural world, I observed an extraordinary thing. I observed that learned men in spectacles were talking of the actual things that happened—dawn and death and so on—as if *they* were rational and inevitable. They talked as if the fact that trees bear fruit were just as *necessary* as the fact that two and one trees make three. But it is not. There is an enormous difference by the test of fairyland; which is the test of the imagination. You cannot *imagine* two and one not making three. But you can easily imagine trees not growing fruit; you can imagine them growing golden candlesticks or tigers hanging on by the tail.

These men in spectacles spoke much of a man named Newton, who was hit by an apple, and who discovered a law.[7] But they could not be got to see the distinction between a true law, a law of reason, and the mere fact of apples falling. If the apple hit Newton's nose, Newton's nose hit the apple. That is a true necessity: because we cannot conceive the one occurring without the other. But we can quite well conceive the apple not falling on his nose; we can fancy it flying ardently through the air to hit some other nose, of which it had a more definite dislike.

We have always in our fairy tales kept this sharp distinction between the science of mental relations, in which there really are laws, and the science of physical facts, in which there are no laws, but only weird repetitions. We believe in bodily miracles, but not in mental impossibilities. We believe that a Beanstalk climbed up to Heaven; but that does not at all confuse our convictions on the philosophical question of how many beans make five.

Here is the peculiar perfection of tone and truth in the nursery tales. The man of science says, "Cut the stalk, and the apple will fall"; but he says it calmly, as if the one idea really led up to the other. The witch in the fairy tale says, "Blow the horn, and the ogre's castle will fall"; but she does not say it as if it were something in which the effect obviously arose out of the cause. Doubtless she has given the advice to many champions, and has seen many castles fall, but she does not lose either her wonder or her reason. She does not muddle her head until it imagines a necessary mental connection between a horn and a falling tower. But the scientific men do muddle their heads, until they imagine a necessary mental connection between an apple leaving the tree and an apple reaching the ground. They do really talk as if they had found not only a set of marvellous facts, but a truth connecting those facts. They do talk as if the connection of two strange things physically connected

---

[7] Chesterton refers to the legend that the famous scientist Isaac Newton (1643–1727) was sitting under an apple tree when an apple fell and hit him on the head, prompting him to describe the law of gravity.

them philosophically. They feel that because one incomprehensible thing constantly follows another incomprehensible thing the two together somehow make up a comprehensible thing. Two black riddles make a white answer.

In fairyland we avoid the word "law"; but in the land of science they are singularly fond of it. Thus they will call some interesting conjecture about how forgotten folks pronounced the alphabet, Grimm's Law.[8] But Grimm's Law is far less intellectual than Grimm's Fairy Tales.[9] The tales are, at any rate, certainly tales; while the law is not a law.

A law implies that we know the nature of the generalisation and enactment; not merely that we have noticed some of the effects. If there is a law that pickpockets shall go to prison, it implies that there is an imaginable mental connection between the idea of prison and the idea of picking pockets. And we know what the idea is. We can say why we take liberty from a man who takes liberties. But we cannot say why an egg can turn into a chicken any more than we can say why a bear could turn into a fairy prince. As *ideas*, the egg and the chicken are further off from each other than the bear and the prince; for no egg in itself suggests a chicken, whereas some princes do suggest bears.

Granted, then, that certain transformations do happen, it is essential that we should regard them in the philosophic manner of fairy tales, not in the unphilosophic manner of science and the "Laws of Nature." When we are asked why eggs turn to birds or fruits fall in autumn, we must answer exactly as the fairy godmother would answer if Cinderella asked her why mice turned to horses or her clothes fell from her at twelve o'clock. We must answer that it is *magic*. It is not a "law," for we do not understand its general

---

[8] Grimm's law is named after Jacob Grimm, who showed changes over time in language, in particular how the Proto-Indo-European stop consonants developed in Proto-Germanic in the first millennium BC.

[9] *Grimm's Fairy Tales* is a collection of fairy tales by Jacob and Wilhelm Grimm, first published in 1812.

formula. It is not a necessity, for though we can count on it happening practically, we have no right to say that it must always happen. It is no argument for unalterable law (as Huxley fancied) that we count on the ordinary course of things. We do not count on it; we bet on it. We risk the remote possibility of a miracle as we do that of a poisoned pancake or a world-destroying comet. We leave it out of account, not because it is a miracle, and therefore an impossibility, but because it is a miracle, and therefore an exception.

All the terms used in the science books, "law," "necessity," "order," "tendency," and so on, are really unintellectual, because they assume an inner synthesis, which we do not possess. The only words that ever satisfied me as describing Nature are the terms used in the fairy books, "charm," "spell," "enchantment." They express the arbitrariness of the fact and its mystery. A tree grows fruit because it is a *magic* tree. Water runs downhill because it is bewitched. The sun shines because it is bewitched.

I deny altogether that this is fantastic or even mystical. We may have some mysticism later on; but this fairy-tale language about things is simply rational and agnostic. It is the only way I can express in words my clear and definite perception that one thing is quite distinct from another; that there is no logical connection between flying and laying eggs.

It is the man who talks about "a law" that he has never seen who is the mystic. Nay, the ordinary scientific man is strictly a sentimentalist. He is a sentimentalist in this essential sense, that he is soaked and swept away by mere associations. He has so often seen birds fly and lay eggs that he feels as if there must be some dreamy, tender connection between the two ideas, whereas there is none. A forlorn lover might be unable to dissociate the moon from lost love; so the materialist is unable to dissociate the moon from the tide. In both cases there is no connection, except that one has seen them together. A sentimentalist might shed tears at the smell of apple-blossom, because, by a dark association of his own, it reminded him of his boyhood. So the materialist professor (though he conceals his tears) is yet a sentimentalist, because, by a dark association of his own, apple-blossoms remind him of apples. But the cool rationalist from fairyland does not see why, in the abstract, the apple tree should not grow crimson tulips; it sometimes does in his country.

The Ancient Instinct of Astonishment

This elementary wonder, however, is not a mere fancy derived from the fairy tales; on the contrary, all the fire of the fairy tales is derived from this. Just as we all like love tales because there is an instinct of sex, we all like astonishing tales because they touch the nerve of the ancient instinct of astonishment.

This is proved by the fact that when we are very young children we do not need fairy tales: we only need tales. Mere life is interesting enough. A child of seven is excited by being told that Tommy opened a door and saw a dragon. But a child of three is excited by being told that Tommy opened a door. Boys like romantic tales; but babies like realistic tales—because they find them romantic. In fact, a baby is about the only person, I should think, to whom a modern realistic novel could be read without boring him.

This proves that even nursery tales only echo an almost prenatal leap of interest and amazement. These tales say that apples were golden only to refresh the forgotten moment when we found that they were green. They make rivers run with wine only to make us remember, for one wild moment, that they run with water. I have said that this is wholly reasonable and even agnostic. And, indeed, on this point I am all for the higher agnosticism; its better name is Ignorance.

We have all read in scientific books, and, indeed, in all romances, the story of the man who has forgotten his name. This man walks about the streets and can see and appreciate everything; only he cannot remember who he is. Well, every man is that man in the story. Every man has forgotten who he is. One may understand the cosmos, but never the ego; the self is more distant than any star. Thou shalt love the Lord thy God; but thou shalt not know thyself. We are all under the same mental calamity; we have all forgotten our names. We have all forgotten what we really are. All that we call common sense and rationality and practicality and positivism only means that for certain dead levels of our life we forget that we have forgotten. All that we call spirit and art and ecstasy only means that for one awful instant we remember that we forget.

Gratitude for Existence

But though (like the man without memory in the novel) we walk the streets with a sort of half-witted admiration, still it is admiration. It is admiration in English and not only admiration in Latin. The wonder has a positive element of praise.

This is the next milestone to be definitely marked on our road through fairyland. I shall speak in the next chapter about optimists and pessimists in their intellectual aspect, so far as they have one. Here I am only trying to describe the enormous emotions which cannot be described. And the strongest emotion was that life was as precious as it was puzzling. It was an ecstasy because it was an adventure; it was an adventure because it was an opportunity. The goodness of the fairy tale was not affected by the fact that there might be more dragons than princesses; it was good to be in a fairy tale.

The test of all happiness is gratitude; and I felt grateful, though I hardly knew to whom. Children are grateful when Santa Claus puts in their stockings gifts of toys or sweets. Could I not be grateful to Santa Claus when he put in my stockings the gift of two miraculous legs? We thank people for birthday presents of cigars and slippers. Can I thank no one for the birthday present of birth?

There were, then, these two first feelings, indefensible and indisputable. The world was a shock, but it was not merely shocking; existence was a surprise, but it was a pleasant surprise. In fact, all my first views were exactly uttered in a riddle that stuck in my brain from boyhood. The question was, "What did the first frog say?" And the answer was, "Lord, how you made me jump!" That says succinctly all that I am saying. God made the frog jump; but the frog prefers jumping. But when these things are settled there enters the second great principle of the fairy philosophy.

The Doctrine of Conditional Joy

Any one can see it who will simply read *Grimm's Fairy Tales* or the fine collections of Mr. Andrew Lang.[10] For the pleasure of pedantry I will call it the Doctrine of Conditional Joy. Touchstone talked of much virtue in an "if";[11] according to elfin ethics all virtue is in an "if."

The note of the fairy utterance always is, "You may live in a palace of gold and sapphire, if you do not say the word 'cow'"; or "You may live happily with the King's daughter, if you do not show her an onion." The vision always hangs upon a veto. All the dizzy and colossal things conceded depend upon one small thing withheld. All the wild and whirling things that are let loose depend upon one thing that is forbidden.

Mr. W. B. Yeats, in his exquisite and piercing elfin poetry, describes the elves as lawless; they plunge in innocent anarchy on the unbridled horses of the air—

Ride on the crest of the dishevelled tide,
And dance upon the mountains like a flame.[12]

It is a dreadful thing to say that Mr. W. B. Yeats does not understand fairyland. But I do say it. He is an ironical Irishman, full of intellectual reactions. He is not stupid enough to understand

---

[10] *The Langs' Fairy Books* were collections, each named after a different color, containing true and fictional stories for children. The books were published between 1889 and 1913 by Andrew Lang, a Scottish man of letters (1844–1912), and his wife, Leonora Blanche Alleyne (1851–1933).

[11] Touchstone is a character in William Shakespeare's play *As You Like It*. He is the court jester of Duke Frederick, the usurper.

[12] William Butler Yeats (1865–1939) was an Irish poet and prominent literary figure of the twentieth century. Chesterton was frequently casual with his quotations. The actual line in Yeats's play *The Land of Heart's Desire* begins "Run on the top . . ."

fairyland. Fairies prefer people of the yokel type like myself; people who gape and grin and do as they are told. Mr. Yeats reads into elfland all the righteous insurrection of his own race. But the lawlessness of Ireland is a Christian lawlessness, founded on reason and justice. The Fenian is rebelling against something he understands only too well;[13] but the true citizen of fairyland is obeying something that he does not understand at all.

In the fairy tale an incomprehensible happiness rests upon an incomprehensible condition. A box is opened, and all evils fly out. A word is forgotten, and cities perish. A lamp is lit, and love flies away. A flower is plucked, and human lives are forfeited. An apple is eaten, and the hope of God is gone.

This is the tone of fairy tales, and it is certainly not lawlessness or even liberty, though men under a mean modern tyranny may think it liberty by comparison. People out of Portland Gaol might think Fleet Street free;[14] but closer study will prove that both fairies and journalists are the slaves of duty.

Fairy godmothers seem at least as strict as other godmothers. Cinderella received a coach out of Wonderland and a coachman out of nowhere, but she received a command—which might have come out of Brixton[15]—that she should be back by twelve. Also, she had a glass slipper; and it cannot be a coincidence that glass is so common a substance in folklore. This princess lives in a glass castle, that princess on a glass hill; this one sees all things in a mirror; they may all live in glass houses if they will not throw stones. For this thin glitter of glass everywhere is the expression of the fact that the happiness is bright but brittle, like the substance most easily smashed by a housemaid or a cat.

---

[13] A "Fenian" refers to a member of a secret revolutionary society—the Fenian Brotherhood and/or the Irish Republican Brotherhood—dedicated to the establishment of an independent Irish Republic in the nineteenth and twentieth centuries.

[14] Portland Gaol refers to a prison. Fleet Street is a major street in London, host to British newspapers from the sixteenth to twentieth centuries.

[15] A district of south London.

And this fairy-tale sentiment also sank into me and became my sentiment towards the whole world. I felt and feel that life itself is as bright as the diamond, but as brittle as the windowpane; and when the heavens were compared to the terrible crystal I can remember a shudder. I was afraid that God would drop the cosmos with a crash.

Remember, however, that to be breakable is not the same as to be perishable. Strike a glass, and it will not endure an instant; simply do not strike it, and it will endure a thousand years. Such, it seemed, was the joy of man, either in elfland or on earth; the happiness depended on *not doing something* which you could at any moment do and which, very often, it was not obvious why you should not do.

Now, the point here is that to *me* this did not seem unjust. If the miller's third son said to the fairy, "Explain why I must not stand on my head in the fairy palace," the other might fairly reply, "Well, if it comes to that, explain the fairy palace."

If Cinderella says, "How is it that I must leave the ball at twelve?" her godmother might answer, "How is it that you are going there till twelve?"

If I leave a man in my will ten talking elephants and a hundred winged horses, he cannot complain if the conditions partake of the slight eccentricity of the gift. He must not look a winged horse in the mouth.

And it seemed to me that existence was itself so very eccentric a legacy that I could not complain of not understanding the limitations of the vision when I did not understand the vision they limited. The frame was no stranger than the picture. The veto might well be as wild as the vision; it might be as startling as the sun, as elusive as the waters, as fantastic and terrible as the towering trees.

For this reason (we may call it the fairy godmother philosophy) I never could join the young men of my time in feeling what they called the general sentiment of *revolt*. I should have resisted, let us hope, any rules that were evil, and with these and their definition I shall deal in another chapter. But I did not feel disposed to resist any rule merely because it was mysterious. Estates are sometimes held by foolish forms, the breaking of a stick or the payment of a peppercorn: I was willing to hold the huge estate of earth and heaven by any such feudal fantasy. It could not well be wilder than the fact that I was allowed to hold it at all.

At this stage I give only one ethical instance to show my meaning. I could never mix in the common murmur of that rising generation against monogamy, because no restriction on sex seemed so odd and unexpected as sex itself. To be allowed, like Endymion, to make love to the moon and then to complain that Jupiter kept his own moons in a harem seemed to me (bred on fairy tales like Endymion's) a vulgar anti-climax.[16] Keeping to one woman is a small price for so much as seeing one woman. To complain that I could only be married once was like complaining that I had only been born once. It was incommensurate with the terrible excitement of which one was talking. It showed, not an exaggerated sensibility to sex, but a curious insensibility to it. A man is a fool who complains that he cannot enter Eden by five gates at once. Polygamy is a lack of the realization of sex; it is like a man plucking five pears in mere absence of mind.

The aesthetes touched the last insane limits of language in their eulogy on lovely things. The thistledown made them weep; a burnished beetle brought them to their knees. Yet their emotion never impressed me for an instant, for this reason, that it never occurred to them to pay for their pleasure in any sort of symbolic sacrifice. Men (I felt) might fast forty days for the sake of hearing a blackbird sing. Men might go through fire to find a cowslip. Yet these lovers of beauty could not even keep sober for the blackbird. They would not go through common Christian marriage by way of recompense to the cowslip. Surely one might pay for extraordinary joy in ordinary morals. Oscar Wilde said that sunsets were not valued because

---

[16] In later Greek mythology, Endymion, a shepherd prince, was suggested by Pliny the Elder as the first human to observe the movements of the moon. The moon goddess fell in love with him. Jupiter is the god of sky and thunder and king of all the gods.

we could not pay for sunsets.[17] But Oscar Wilde was wrong; we can pay for sunsets. We can pay for them by not being Oscar Wilde.

Necessity and Repetition

Well, I left the fairy tales lying on the floor of the nursery, and I have not found any books so sensible since. I left the nurse guardian of tradition and democracy, and I have not found any modern type so sanely radical or so sanely conservative. But the matter for important comment was here: that when I first went out into the mental atmosphere of the modern world, I found that the modern world was positively opposed on two points to my nurse and to the nursery tales. It has taken me a long time to find out that the modern world is wrong and my nurse was right. The really curious thing was this: that modern thought contradicted this basic creed of my boyhood on its two most essential doctrines.

I have explained that the fairy tales founded in me two convictions; first, that this world is a wild and startling place, which might have been quite different, but which is quite delightful; second, that before this wildness and delight one may well be modest and submit to the queerest limitations of so queer a kindness. But I found the whole modern world running like a high tide against both my tendernesses; and the shock of that collision created two sudden and spontaneous sentiments, which I have had ever since and which, crude as they were, have since hardened into convictions.

First, I found the whole modern world talking scientific fatalism; saying that everything is as it must always have been, being unfolded without fault from the beginning. The leaf on the tree is green because it could never have been anything else.

Now, the fairy-tale philosopher is glad that the leaf is green precisely because it might have been scarlet. He feels as if it had turned green an instant before he looked at it. He is pleased that snow is white on the strictly reasonable ground that it might have been

[17] Oscar Wilde (1854–1900) was an Irish poet and playwright.

black. Every colour has in it a bold quality as of choice; the red of garden roses is not only decisive but dramatic, like suddenly spilt blood. He feels that something has been *done.*

But the great determinists of the nineteenth century were strongly against this native feeling that something had happened an instant before. In fact, according to them, nothing ever really had happened since the beginning of the world. Nothing ever had happened since existence had happened; and even about the date of that they were not very sure.

The modern world as I found it was solid for modern Calvinism, for the necessity of things being as they are. But when I came to ask them I found they had really no proof of this unavoidable repetition in things except the fact that the things were repeated. Now, the mere repetition made the things to me rather more weird than more rational.

It was as if, having seen a curiously shaped nose in the street and dismissed it as an accident, I had then seen six other noses of the same astonishing shape. I should have fancied for a moment that it must be some local secret society. So one elephant having a trunk was odd; but all elephants having trunks looked like a plot. I speak here only of an emotion, and of an emotion at once stubborn and subtle.

But the repetition in Nature seemed sometimes to be an excited repetition, like that of an angry schoolmaster saying the same thing over and over again. The grass seemed signalling to me with all its fingers at once; the crowded stars seemed bent upon being understood. The sun would make me see him if he rose a thousand times. The recurrences of the universe rose to the maddening rhythm of an incantation, and I began to see an idea.

All the towering materialism which dominates the modern mind rests ultimately upon one assumption; a false assumption. It is supposed that if a thing goes on repeating itself it is probably dead; a piece of clockwork. People feel that if the universe was personal it would vary; if the sun were alive it would dance.

This is a fallacy even in relation to known fact. For the variation in human affairs is generally brought into them, not by life, but by death; by the dying down or breaking off of their strength or desire. A man varies his movements because of some slight element of failure or fatigue. He gets into an omnibus because he is tired of walking; or he walks because he is tired of sitting still. But if his life and joy were so gigantic that he never tired of going to Islington, he might go to Islington as regularly as the Thames goes to Sheerness.[18] The very speed and ecstasy of his life would have the stillness of death. The sun rises every morning. I do not rise every morning; but the variation is due not to my activity, but to my inaction.

Now, to put the matter in a popular phrase, it might be true that the sun rises regularly because he never gets tired of rising. His routine might be due, not to a lifelessness, but to a rush of life. The thing I mean can be seen, for instance, in children, when they find some game or joke that they specially enjoy. A child kicks his legs rhythmically through excess, not absence, of life. Because children have abounding vitality, because they are in spirit fierce and free, therefore they want things repeated and unchanged. They always say, "Do it again"; and the grown-up person does it again until he is nearly dead. For grown-up people are not strong enough to exult in monotony. But perhaps God is strong enough to exult in monotony. It is possible that God says every morning, "Do it again" to the sun; and every evening, "Do it again" to the moon. It may not be automatic necessity that makes all daisies alike; it may be that God makes every daisy separately, but has never got tired of making them. It may be that He has the eternal appetite of infancy; for we have sinned and grown old, and our Father is younger than we.

---

[18] Islington is a mainly residential district of inner London. The River Thames flows through southern England, including London. Sheerness is a town beside the mouth of the River Medway.

The repetition in Nature may not be a mere recurrence; it may be a theatrical *encore*. Heaven may *encore* the bird who laid an egg. If the human being conceives and brings forth a human child instead of bringing forth a fish, or a bat, or a griffin, the reason may not be that we are fixed in an animal fate without life or purpose. It may be that our little tragedy has touched the gods, that they admire it from their starry galleries, and that at the end of every human drama man is called again and again before the curtain. Repetition may go on for millions of years, by mere choice, and at any instant it may stop. Man may stand on the earth generation after generation, and yet each birth be his positively last appearance.

This was my first conviction; made by the shock of my childish emotions meeting the modern creed in mid-career. I had always vaguely felt facts to be miracles in the sense that they are wonderful: now I began to think them miracles in the stricter sense that they were *willful*. I mean that they were, or might be, repeated exercises of some will. In short, I had always believed that the world involved magic: now I thought that perhaps it involved a magician. And this pointed a profound emotion always present and subconscious; that this world of ours has some purpose; and if there is a purpose, there is a person. I had always felt life first as a story: and if there is a story there is a storyteller.

The Size of the Universe

But modern thought also hit my second human tradition. It went against the fairy feeling about strict limits and conditions. The one thing it loved to talk about was expansion and largeness. Herbert Spencer would have been greatly annoyed if any one had called him an imperialist,[19] and therefore it is highly regrettable that nobody did. But he was an imperialist of the lowest type. He popularized

---

[19] Herbert Spencer (1820–1903) was an English philosopher and biologist, most known for his view of social Darwinism.

this contemptible notion that the size of the solar system ought to over-awe the spiritual dogma of man.

Why should a man surrender his dignity to the solar system any more than to a whale? If mere size proves that man is not the image of God, then a whale may be the image of God; a somewhat formless image; what one might call an impressionist portrait. It is quite futile to argue that man is small compared to the cosmos; for man was always small compared to the nearest tree.

But Herbert Spencer, in his headlong imperialism, would insist that we had in some way been conquered and annexed by the astronomical universe. He spoke about men and their ideals exactly as the most insolent Unionist talks about the Irish and their ideals.[20] He turned mankind into a small nationality. And his evil influence can be seen even in the most spirited and honourable of later scientific authors; notably in the early romances of Mr. H. G. Wells. Many moralists have in an exaggerated way represented the earth as wicked. But Mr. Wells and his school made the heavens wicked. We should lift up our eyes to the stars from whence would come our ruin.[21]

But the expansion of which I speak was much more evil than all this. I have remarked that the materialist, like the madman, is in prison; in the prison of one thought. These people seemed to think it singularly inspiring to keep on saying that the prison was very large. The size of this scientific universe gave one no novelty, no relief. The cosmos went on forever, but not in its wildest constellation could there be anything really interesting; anything, for instance, such as forgiveness or free will. The grandeur or infinity of the secret of its cosmos added nothing to it. It was like telling a prisoner in Reading gaol that he would be glad to hear that

---

[20] A member of the political party advocating union between Ireland and Great Britain, in opposition to Irish home rule.

[21] This is a twist on Psalm 121:1: "I will lift up mine eyes unto the hills, from whence cometh my help."

the gaol now covered half the county.[22] The warder would have nothing to show the man except more and more long corridors of stone lit by ghastly lights and empty of all that is human. So these expanders of the universe had nothing to show us except more and more infinite corridors of space lit by ghastly suns and empty of all that is divine.

In fairyland there had been a real law; a law that could be broken, for the definition of a law is something that can be broken. But the machinery of this cosmic prison was something that could not be broken; for we ourselves were only a part of its machinery. We were either unable to do things or we were destined to do them. The idea of the mystical condition quite disappeared; one can neither have the firmness of keeping laws nor the fun of breaking them. The largeness of this universe had nothing of that freshness and airy outbreak which we have praised in the universe of the poet. This modern universe is literally an empire; that is, it was vast, but it is not free. One went into larger and larger windowless rooms, rooms big with Babylonian perspective; but one never found the smallest window or a whisper of outer air.

Their infernal parallels seemed to expand with distance; but for me all good things come to a point, swords for instance. So finding the boast of the big cosmos so unsatisfactory to my emotions I began to argue about it a little; and I soon found that the whole attitude was even shallower than could have been expected. According to these people the cosmos was one thing since it had one unbroken rule. Only (they would say) while it is one thing, it is also the only thing there is. Why, then, should one worry particularly to call it large? There is nothing to compare it with. It would be just as sensible to call it small.

A man may say, "I like this vast cosmos, with its throng of stars and its crowd of varied creatures." But if it comes to that why should

---

[22] Reading gaol was a prison in Reading.

not a man say, "I like this cosy little cosmos, with its decent number of stars and as neat a provision of live stock as I wish to see"?

One is as good as the other; they are both mere sentiments. It is mere sentiment to rejoice that the sun is larger than the earth; it is quite as sane a sentiment to rejoice that the sun is no larger than it is. A man chooses to have an emotion about the largeness of the world; why should he not choose to have an emotion about its smallness?

It happened that I had that emotion. When one is fond of anything one addresses it by diminutives, even if it is an elephant or a life-guardsman. The reason is, that anything, however huge, that can be conceived of as complete, can be conceived of as small. If military moustaches did not suggest a sword or tusks a tail, then the object would be vast because it would be immeasurable. But the moment you can imagine a guardsman you can imagine a small guardsman. The moment you really see an elephant you can call it "Tiny." If you can make a statue of a thing you can make a statuette of it.

These people professed that the universe was one coherent thing; but they were not fond of the universe. But I was frightfully fond of the universe and wanted to address it by a diminutive. I often did so; and it never seemed to mind.

Actually and in truth I did feel that these dim dogmas of vitality were better expressed by calling the world small than by calling it large. For about infinity there was a sort of carelessness which was the reverse of the fierce and pious care which I felt touching the pricelessness and the peril of life. They showed only a dreary waste; but I felt a sort of sacred thrift. For economy is far more romantic than extravagance. To them stars were an unending income of halfpence; but I felt about the golden sun and the silver moon as a schoolboy feels if he has one sovereign and one shilling.[23]

---

[23] The sovereign is a gold coin of the United Kingdom, valued at one pound sterling. The shilling was a silver coin in use until 1971, worth one-twentieth of a pound sterling.

Saved from a Wreck

These subconscious convictions are best hit off by the colour and tone of certain tales. Thus I have said that stories of magic alone can express my sense that life is not only a pleasure but a kind of eccentric privilege.

I may express this other feeling of cosmic cosiness by allusion to another book always read in boyhood, *Robinson Crusoe,*[24] which I read about this time, and which owes its eternal vivacity to the fact that it celebrates the poetry of limits, nay, even the wild romance of prudence. Crusoe is a man on a small rock with a few comforts just snatched from the sea: the best thing in the book is simply the list of things saved from the wreck. The greatest of poems is an inventory. Every kitchen tool becomes ideal because Crusoe might have dropped it in the sea. It is a good exercise, in empty or ugly hours of the day, to look at anything, the coalscuttle or the bookcase, and think how happy one could be to have brought it out of the sinking ship on to the solitary island.

But it is a better exercise still to remember how all things have had this hair-breadth escape: everything has been saved from a wreck. Every man has had one horrible adventure: as a hidden untimely birth he had not been, as infants that never see the light. Men spoke much in my boyhood of restricted or ruined men of genius: and it was common to say that many a man was a Great Might-Have-Been. To me it is a more solid and startling fact that any man in the street is a Great Might-Not-Have-Been.

But I really felt (the fancy may seem foolish) as if all the order and number of things were the romantic remnant of Crusoe's ship. That there are two sexes and one sun, was like the fact that there were two guns and one axe. It was poignantly urgent that none should be lost; but somehow, it was rather fun that none could be added. The trees and the planets seemed like things saved from

[24] A novel by Daniel Defoe, first published in 1719, that tells the tale of a castaway on a remote tropical desert island for twenty-eight years.

the wreck: and when I saw the Matterhorn I was glad that it had not been overlooked in the confusion.[25] I felt economical about the stars as if they were sapphires (they are called so in Milton's Eden): I hoarded the hills. For the universe is a single jewel, and while it is a natural cant to talk of a jewel as peerless and priceless, of this jewel it is literally true. This cosmos is indeed without peer and without price: for there cannot be another one.

Summing Up My Attitude toward Life

Thus ends, in unavoidable inadequacy, the attempt to utter the unutterable things. These are my ultimate attitudes towards life; the soils for the seeds of doctrine. These in some dark way I thought before I could write, and felt before I could think: that we may proceed more easily afterwards, I will roughly recapitulate them now.

I felt in my bones; first, that this world does not explain itself. It may be a miracle with a supernatural explanation; it may be a conjuring trick, with a natural explanation. But the explanation of the conjuring trick, if it is to satisfy me, will have to be better than the natural explanations I have heard. The thing is magic, true or false.

Second, I came to feel as if magic must have a meaning, and meaning must have someone to mean it. There was something personal in the world, as in a work of art; whatever it meant it meant violently.

Third, I thought this purpose beautiful in its old design, in spite of its defects, such as dragons.

Fourth, that the proper form of thanks to it is some form of humility and restraint: we should thank God for beer and Burgundy by not drinking too much of them. We owed, also, an obedience to whatever made us.

---

[25] The Matterhorn is a mountain of the Alps.

And last, and strangest, there had come into my mind a vague and vast impression that in some way all good was a remnant to be stored and held sacred out of some primordial ruin. Man had saved his good as Crusoe saved his goods: he had saved them from a wreck.

All this I felt and the age gave me no encouragement to feel it. And all this time I had not even thought of Christian theology.

Chapter Summary

Chesterton began this chapter with something of a digression—an explanation of why he is a Liberal who believes in democracy. He started with a defense of popular tradition, including men and women of the past, in order to show how the common sense of fairyland, spread through storytelling to children, tells us something true about the world we live in.

At the end of this chapter, Chesterton summed up his argument in five points. First, he showed that the world does not explain itself. We need someone or something else to explain it to us (hence, the nursery). Second, he insisted that the magic and wonder in the world mean something; and if it means something, there must be someone to mean it. Third, he claimed that the purpose of the created world is beautiful in its design. Far from being something merely mechanical and lifeless, the world is teeming with life and energy, abounding in magic. Fourth, he helped us see that our response should be gratitude and humility ("the fairy godmother philosophy") at this wondrous creation that has come to us as a gift. Lastly, he noticed that there's a sense in which we have been saved from a primordial ruin. Everything that is good seems to be a remnant from something much better.

Discussion Questions

1. How does Chesterton's approach of valuing the opinions of people in the past ("the democracy of the dead") differ from many people in our society today?
2. How might fairy tales help us recapture a sense of wonder at our world?
3. Why is Chesterton so opposed to the idea that the world is here by logical necessity, ruled by mechanical laws of nature?
4. Why should our astonishment at the world engender feelings of gratitude and humility?

5. In what ways does our appreciation of the world increase when we think of all we see as having been saved from a shipwreck?

FIVE

This chapter marks the turning point in Chesterton's intellectual journey toward Christianity—the precise moment when he first discovers that the Christian tradition is the key that makes sense of these tensions present in his outlook on the world. The key fits the lock, and "all the other parts fitted and fell in with an eerie exactitude," he wrote, an analogy that he will explore in greater detail in the next chapter. For now, you'll see how Chesterton came to realize that God is personal, that he made a world distinct from himself, and the implications of that distinction for the philosophy that Chesterton believes to make most sense of the world.

Chesterton's goal in this chapter is to take the main point from the previous chapter—the idea that ethics must be grounded in gratitude—and set it within the framework of faith and reason he laid out in earlier chapters. In so doing, he will contrast the optimist and the pessimist, and he will make the case that the proper approach to the world is to hate it and love it at the same time—to hate what needs changing and to love it enough to want to see it better. The proper response is a deep-seated patriotic loyalty to the world as good, alongside the realization that the world is fallen and requires reform. Christianity avoids the twin errors of looking inward and finding God within yourself, or looking outward and mistaking Nature for God.

Memorable Parts to Look For

- The need for primary loyalty to the world combined with a desire to reform it
- Chesterton's distinction between martyrdom and suicide
- The imbecility of deciding on a philosophy based on "the clock"—what one can believe in one age but not in another
- The answer to why we can feel "homesick at home"

THE FLAG OF THE WORLD

When I was a boy there were two curious men running about who were called the optimist and the pessimist. I constantly used the words myself, but I cheerfully confess that I never had any very special idea of what they meant. The only thing which might be considered evident was that they could not mean what they said; for the ordinary verbal explanation was that the optimist thought this world as good as it could be, while the pessimist thought it as bad as it could be. Both these statements being obviously raving nonsense, one had to cast about for other explanations. An optimist could not mean a man who thought everything right and nothing wrong. For that is meaningless; it is like calling everything right and nothing left.

Upon the whole, I came to the conclusion that the optimist thought everything good except the pessimist, and that the pessimist thought everything bad, except himself. It would be unfair to omit altogether from the list the mysterious but suggestive definition said to have been given by a little girl, "An optimist is a man who looks after your eyes, and a pessimist is a man who looks after your feet." I am not sure that this is not the best definition of all. There is even a sort of allegorical truth in it. For there might, perhaps, be a profitable distinction drawn between that more dreary thinker who thinks merely of our contact with the earth from moment to moment, and that happier thinker who considers rather our primary power of vision and of choice of road.

But this is a deep mistake in this alternative of the optimist and the pessimist. The assumption of it is that a man criticises this world as if he were house-hunting, as if he were being shown over a new suite of apartments. If a man came to this world from some other world in full possession of his powers he might discuss whether the advantage of midsummer woods made up for the disadvantage of mad dogs, just as a man looking for lodgings might balance the presence of a telephone against the absence of a sea view. But no man is in that position. A man belongs to this world before he begins to ask if it is nice to belong to it. He has fought for the flag, and often won heroic victories for the flag long before he has ever enlisted. To put shortly what seems the essential matter, he has a loyalty long before he has any admiration.

Optimists, Pessimists, and the Question of Cosmic Loyalty

In the last chapter it has been said that the primary feeling that this world is strange and yet attractive is best expressed in fairy tales. The reader may, if he likes, put down the next stage to that bellicose and even jingo literature which commonly comes next in the history of a boy.[1] We all owe much sound morality to the penny dreadfuls.[2]

Whatever the reason, it seemed and still seems to me that our attitude towards life can be better expressed in terms of a kind of military loyalty than in terms of criticism and approval. My acceptance of the universe is not optimism, it is more like patriotism. It

---

[1] *Jingo* means "patriotic."

[2] Cheap, popular serial literature produced in the UK in the 1800s. The term comes from the fact that new parts of the story were published weekly, each costing a penny.

is a matter of primary loyalty. The world is not a lodging house at Brighton, which we are to leave because it is miserable. It is the fortress of our family, with the flag flying on the turret, and the more miserable it is the less we should leave it.

The point is not that this world is too sad to love or too glad not to love; the point is that when you do love a thing, its gladness is a reason for loving it, and its sadness a reason for loving it more. All optimistic thoughts about England and all pessimistic thoughts about her are alike reasons for the English patriot. Similarly, optimism and pessimism are alike arguments for the cosmic patriot.

Optimism and the Cosmic Patriot

Let us suppose we are confronted with a desperate thing—say Pimlico.[3] If we think what is really best for Pimlico we shall find the thread of thought leads to the throne or the mystic and the arbitrary. It is not enough for a man to disapprove of Pimlico: in that case he will merely cut his throat or move to Chelsea.[4] Nor, certainly, is it enough for a man to approve of Pimlico: for then it will remain Pimlico, which would be awful. The only way out of it seems to be for somebody to love Pimlico: to love it with a transcendental tie and without any earthly reason. If there arose a man who loved Pimlico, then Pimlico would rise into ivory towers and golden pinnacles; Pimlico would attire herself as a woman does when she is loved. For decoration is not given to hide horrible things: but to decorate things already adorable. A mother does not give her child a blue bow because he is so ugly without it. A lover does not give a girl a necklace to hide her neck. If men loved Pimlico as mothers love children, arbitrarily, because it is *theirs*, Pimlico in a year or two might be fairer than Florence.

---

[3] An area in central London west of Westminster, bounded by the River Thames to the south.

[4] An area of southwest London.

Some readers will say that this is a mere fantasy. I answer that this is the actual history of mankind. This, as a fact, is how cities did grow great. Go back to the darkest roots of civilization and you will find them knotted round some sacred stone or encircling some sacred well. People first paid honour to a spot and afterwards gained glory for it. Men did not love Rome because she was great. She was great because they had loved her.

The eighteenth-century theories of the social contract have been exposed to much clumsy criticism in our time; insofar as they meant that there is at the back of all historic government an idea of content and cooperation, they were demonstrably right. But they really were wrong, insofar as they suggested that men had ever aimed at order or ethics directly by a conscious exchange of interests.

Morality did not begin by one man saying to another, "I will not hit you if you do not hit me"; there is no trace of such a transaction. There *is* a trace of both men having said, "We must not hit each other in the holy place." They gained their morality by guarding their religion. They did not cultivate courage. They fought for the shrine, and found they had become courageous. They did not cultivate cleanliness. They purified themselves for the altar, and found that they were clean.

The history of the Jews is the only early document known to most Englishmen, and the facts can be judged sufficiently from that. The Ten Commandments which have been found substantially common to mankind were merely military commands; a code of regimental orders, issued to protect a certain ark across a certain desert. Anarchy was evil because it endangered the sanctity. And only when they made a holy day for God did they find they had made a holiday for men.

Pessimism and the Anti-Patriot

If it be granted that this primary devotion to a place or thing is a source of creative energy, we can pass on to a very peculiar fact. Let us reiterate for an instant that the only right optimism is a sort of universal patriotism. What is the matter with the pessimist? I think it can be stated by saying that he is the cosmic anti-patriot. And what is the matter with the anti-patriot? I think it can be stated, without undue bitterness, by saying that he is the candid friend. And what is the matter with the candid friend? There we strike the rock of real life and immutable human nature.

I venture to say that what is bad in the candid friend is simply that he is not candid. He is keeping something back—his own gloomy pleasure in saying unpleasant things. He has a secret desire to hurt, not merely to help. This is certainly, I think, what makes a certain sort of anti-patriot irritating to healthy citizens.

I do not speak (of course) of the anti-patriotism which only irritates feverish stockbrokers and gushing actresses; that is only patriotism speaking plainly. A man who says that no patriot should attack the Boer War until it is over is not worth answering intelligently;[5] he is saying that no good son should warn his mother off a cliff until she has fallen over it.

But there is an anti-patriot who honestly angers honest men, and the explanation of him is, I think, what I have suggested: he is the uncandid candid friend; the man who says, "I am sorry to say we are ruined," and is not sorry at all. And he may be said, without rhetoric, to be a traitor; for he is using that ugly knowledge which was allowed him to strengthen the army, to discourage people from joining it. Because he is allowed to be pessimistic as a military adviser he is being pessimistic as a recruiting sergeant. Just in the same way the pessimist (who is the cosmic anti-patriot) uses the freedom that life allows to her counsellors to lure away the people from her flag. Granted that he states only facts, it is still essential to know what

---

[5] The Boer War (1899–1902) began when Britain, in the desire for gold, attempted to take over the small South African country of Transvaal. The Boers, descendants of the Dutch and Germans who had settled there, were mostly farmers. Chesterton disagreed with the premise of the war. As someone who loved his own land, he sympathized with the patriotic feelings of people in other countries who resisted British imperialism.

are his emotions, what is his motive. It may be that twelve hundred men in Tottenham are down with smallpox; but we want to know whether this is stated by some great philosopher who wants to curse the gods, or only by some common clergyman who wants to help the men.

Optimism and the Road to Reform

The evil of the pessimist is, then, not that he chastises gods and men, but that he does not love what he chastises—he has not this primary and supernatural loyalty to things. What is the evil of the man commonly called an optimist? Obviously, it is felt that the optimist, wishing to defend the honour of this world, will defend the indefensible. He is the jingo of the universe; he will say, "My cosmos, right or wrong." He will be less inclined to the reform of things; more inclined to a sort of front-bench official answer to all attacks, soothing every one with assurances. He will not wash the world, but whitewash the world. All this (which is true of a type of optimist) leads us to the one really interesting point of psychology, which could not be explained without it.

We say there must be a primal loyalty to life: the only question is, shall it be a natural or a supernatural loyalty? If you like to put it so, shall it be a reasonable or an unreasonable loyalty? Now, the extraordinary thing is that the bad optimism (the whitewashing, the weak defence of everything) comes in with the reasonable optimism. Rational optimism leads to stagnation: it is irrational optimism that leads to reform.

Let me explain by using once more the parallel of patriotism. The man who is most likely to ruin the place he loves is exactly the man who loves it with a reason. The man who will improve the place is the man who loves it without a reason. If a man loves some feature of Pimlico (which seems unlikely), he may find himself defending that feature against Pimlico itself. But if he simply loves Pimlico itself, he may lay it waste and turn it into the New Jerusalem.

I do not deny that reform may be excessive; I only say that it is the mystic patriot who reforms. Mere jingo self-contentment is commonest among those who have some pedantic reason for their patriotism. The worst jingoes do not love England, but a theory of England. If we love England for being an empire, we may overrate the success with which we rule the Hindus. But if we love it only for being a nation, we can face all events: for it would be a nation even if the Hindus ruled us.

Thus also only those will permit their patriotism to falsify history whose patriotism depends on history. A man who loves England for being English will not mind how she arose. But a man who loves England for being Anglo-Saxon may go against all facts for his fancy. He may end (like Carlyle and Freeman[6]) by maintaining that the Norman Conquest was a Saxon Conquest. He may end in utter unreason—because he has a reason. A man who loves France for being military will palliate the army of 1870. But a man who loves France for being France will improve the army of 1870. This is exactly what the French have done, and France is a good instance of the working paradox. Nowhere else is patriotism more purely abstract and arbitrary; and nowhere else is reform more drastic and sweeping. The more transcendental is your patriotism, the more practical are your politics.

Perhaps the most everyday instance of this point is in the case of women; and their strange and strong loyalty. Some stupid people started the idea that because women obviously back up their own people through everything, therefore women are blind and do not see anything. They can hardly have known any women. The same women who are ready to defend their men through thick and thin

[6] Thomas Carlyle (1795–1881) was a British writer and historian. Edward Augustus Freeman (1823–92) was an English historian whose book *The History of the Norman Conquest of England* argued that the character of the English population was not fundamentally changed by the conquest.

are (in their personal intercourse with the man) almost morbidly lucid about the thinness of his excuses or the thickness of his head.

A man's friend likes him but leaves him as he is: his wife loves him and is always trying to turn him into somebody else. Women who are utter mystics in their creed are utter cynics in their criticism. Thackeray expressed this well when he made Pendennis' mother, who worshipped her son as a god, yet assume that he would go wrong as a man.[7] She underrated his virtue, though she overrated his value. The devotee is entirely free to criticise; the fanatic can safely be a sceptic. Love is not blind; that is the last thing that it is. Love is bound; and the more it is bound the less it is blind.

This at least had come to be my position about all that was called optimism, pessimism, and improvement. Before any cosmic act of reform we must have a cosmic oath of allegiance. A man must be interested in life, then he could be disinterested in his views of it. "My son give me thy heart"; the heart must be fixed on the right thing: the moment we have a fixed heart we have a free hand.

The Riddle: Love and Hate for the World

I must pause to anticipate an obvious criticism. It will be said that a rational person accepts the world as mixed of good and evil with a decent satisfaction and a decent endurance. But this is exactly the attitude which I maintain to be defective.

It is, I know, very common in this age; it was perfectly put in those quiet lines of Matthew Arnold which are more piercingly blasphemous than the shrieks of Schopenhauer—

Enough we live:—and if a life,
With large results so little rife,

---

[7] William Thackeray (1811–63) was an Indian-born English novelist. Chesterton is referring to the main character in *The History of Pendennis: His Fortunes and Misfortunes, His Friends and His Greatest Enemy*, a novel about a young English gentleman born in the country who set out for London to find his place in society.

Though bearable, seem hardly worth
This pomp of worlds,
this pain of birth.[8]

I know this feeling fills our epoch, and I think it freezes our epoch. For our Titanic purposes of faith and revolution, what we need is not the cold acceptance of the world as a compromise, but some way in which we can heartily hate and heartily love it. We do not want joy and anger to neutralize each other and produce a surly contentment; we want a fiercer delight and a fiercer discontent. We have to feel the universe at once as an ogre's castle, to be stormed, and yet as our own cottage, to which we can return at evening.

No one doubts that an ordinary man can get on with this world: but we demand not strength enough to get on with it, but strength enough to get it on. Can he hate it enough to change it, and yet love it enough to think it worth changing? Can he look up at its colossal good without once feeling acquiescence? Can he look up at its colossal evil without once feeling despair? Can he, in short, be at once not only a pessimist and an optimist, but a fanatical pessimist and a fanatical optimist? Is he enough of a pagan to die for the world, and enough of a Christian to die to it? In this combination, I maintain, it is the rational optimist who fails, the irrational optimist who succeeds. He is ready to smash the whole universe for the sake of itself.

The Sin of Suicide

I put these things not in their mature logical sequence, but as they came: and this view was cleared and sharpened by an accident of the time. Under the lengthening shadow of Ibsen,[9] an argument

---

[8] Matthew Arnold (1822–88) was an English poet and cultural critic. Chesterton is quoting from Arnold's poem "Resignation."

[9] Henrik Ibsen (1828–1906) was a Norwegian playwright, known today as "the father of realism."

arose whether it was not a very nice thing to murder one's self.[10] Grave moderns told us that we must not even say "poor fellow," of a man who had blown his brains out, since he was an enviable person, and had only blown them out because of their exceptional excellence. Mr. William Archer even suggested that in the golden age there would be penny-in-the-slot machines, by which a man could kill himself for a penny.[11]

In all this I found myself utterly hostile to many who called themselves liberal and humane. Not only is suicide a sin, it is the sin. It is the ultimate and absolute evil, the refusal to take an interest in existence; the refusal to take the oath of loyalty to life. The man who kills a man, kills a man. The man who kills himself, kills all men; as far as he is concerned he wipes out the world. His act is worse (symbolically considered) than any rape or dynamite outrage. For it destroys all buildings: it insults all women. The thief is satisfied with diamonds; but the suicide is not: that is his crime. He cannot be bribed, even by the blazing stones of the Celestial City.[12] The thief compliments the things he steals, if not the owner of them. But the suicide insults everything on earth by not stealing it. He defiles every flower by refusing to live for its sake. There is not a tiny creature in the cosmos at whom his death is not a sneer. When a man hangs himself on a tree, the leaves might fall off in anger and the birds fly away in fury: for each has received a personal affront.

Of course there may be pathetic emotional excuses for the act. There often are for rape, and there almost always are for dynamite. But if it comes to clear ideas and the intelligent meaning of things, then there is much more rational and philosophic truth in the burial at the cross-roads and the stake driven through the body,

---

[10] Chesterton is referring to a movement that glorified suicide during the last decades of the nineteenth century.

[11] William Archer (1856–1924) was a Scottish writer and an early advocate and translator of the plays of Henrik Ibsen. He also supported George Bernard Shaw.

[12] The Christian pilgrim's goal, another way of speaking of heaven, in John Bunyan's *Pilgrim's Progress*.

than in Mr. Archer's suicidal automatic machines. There is a meaning in burying the suicide apart. The man's crime is different from other crimes—for it makes even crimes impossible.

Suicide vs. Martyrdom

About the same time I read a solemn flippancy by some free thinker: he said that a suicide was only the same as a martyr. The open fallacy of this helped to clear the question. Obviously a suicide is the opposite of a martyr. A martyr is a man who cares so much for something outside him, that he forgets his own personal life. A suicide is a man who cares so little for anything outside him, that he wants to see the last of everything. One wants something to begin: the other wants everything to end.

In other words, the martyr is noble, exactly because (however he renounces the world or execrates all humanity) he confesses this ultimate link with life; he sets his heart outside himself: he dies that something may live. The suicide is ignoble because he has not this link with being: he is a mere destroyer; spiritually, he destroys the universe.

And then I remembered the stake and the crossroads, and the queer fact that Christianity had shown this weird harshness to the suicide. For Christianity had shown a wild encouragement of the martyr. Historic Christianity was accused, not entirely without reason, of carrying martyrdom and asceticism to a point, desolate and pessimistic. The early Christian martyrs talked of death with a horrible happiness. They blasphemed the beautiful duties of the body: they smelt the grave afar off like a field of flowers. All this has seemed to many the very poetry of pessimism. Yet there is the stake at the crossroads to show what Christianity thought of the pessimist.

This was the first of the long train of enigmas with which Christianity entered the discussion. And there went with it a peculiarity of which I shall have to speak more markedly, as a note of all Christian notions, but which distinctly began in this one. The Christian attitude to the martyr and the suicide was not what is so often affirmed in modern morals. It was not a matter of degree. It was not that a line must be drawn somewhere, and that the self-slayer in exaltation fell within the line, the self-slayer in sadness just beyond it. The Christian feeling evidently was not merely that the suicide was carrying martyrdom too far. The Christian feeling was furiously for one and furiously against the other: these two things that looked so much alike were at opposite ends of heaven and hell. One man flung away his life; he was so good that his dry bones could heal cities in pestilence. Another man flung away life; he was so bad that his bones would pollute his brethren's. I am not saying this fierceness was right; but why was it so fierce?

Christianity as the Answer to a Riddle

Here it was that I first found that my wandering feet were in some beaten track. Christianity had also felt this opposition of the martyr to the suicide: had it perhaps felt it for the same reason? Had Christianity felt what I felt, but could not (and cannot) express—this need for a first loyalty to things, and then for a ruinous reform of things?

Then I remembered that it was actually the charge against Christianity that it combined these two things which I was wildly trying to combine. Christianity was accused, at one and the same time, of being too optimistic about the universe and of being too pessimistic about the world. The coincidence made me suddenly stand still.

Christianity's View of the World

An imbecile habit has arisen in modern controversy of saying that such and such a creed can be held in one age but cannot be held in another. Some dogma, we are told, was credible in the twelfth century, but is not credible in the twentieth. You might as well say that a certain philosophy can be believed on Mondays, but cannot be believed on Tuesdays. You might as well say of a view of the cosmos that it was suitable to half-past three, but not suitable to half-past four. What a man can believe depends upon his philosophy, not upon the clock or the century. If a man believes in unalterable natural law, he cannot believe in any miracle in any age. If a man believes in a will behind law, he can believe in any miracle in any age.

Suppose, for the sake of argument, we are concerned with a case of thaumaturgic healing.[13] A materialist of the twelfth century could not believe it any more than a materialist of the twentieth century. But a Christian Scientist of the twentieth century can believe it as much as a Christian of the twelfth century.[14] It is simply a matter of a man's theory of things. Therefore in dealing with any historical answer, the point is not whether it was given in our time, but whether it was given in answer to our question. And the more I thought about when and how Christianity had come into the world, the more I felt that it had actually come to answer this question.

It is commonly the loose and latitudinarian Christians who pay quite indefensible compliments to Christianity. They talk as if there had never been any piety or pity until Christianity came, a point on which any mediaeval would have been eager to correct them. They represent that the remarkable thing about Christianity was that it was the first to preach simplicity or self-restraint, or inwardness and sincerity. They will think me very narrow (whatever that means) if I say that the remarkable thing about Christianity was that it was the first to preach Christianity. Its peculiarity was that it was peculiar, and simplicity and sincerity are not peculiar, but obvious ideals for all mankind. Christianity was the answer to a riddle, not the last truism uttered after a long talk.

---

[13] Thaumaturgy refers to a magician's work of magic or a saint's ability to perform miracles.

[14] A Christian Scientist is an adherent of Christian Science and its founder Mary Baker Eddy, who taught that reality is purely spiritual and disease is in the mind, not a physical disorder.

Christianity against the Inner Light

Only the other day I saw in an excellent weekly paper of Puritan tone this remark, that Christianity when stripped of its armour of dogma (as who should speak of a man stripped of his armour of bones), turned out to be nothing but the Quaker doctrine of the Inner Light.[15] Now, if I were to say that Christianity came into the world specially to destroy the doctrine of the Inner Light, that would be an exaggeration. But it would be very much nearer to the truth.

The last Stoics, like Marcus Aurelius, were exactly the people who did believe in the Inner Light.[16] Their dignity, their weariness, their sad external care for others, their incurable internal care for themselves, were all due to the Inner Light, and existed only by that dismal illumination. Notice that Marcus Aurelius insists, as such introspective moralists always do, upon small things done or undone; it is because he has not hate or love enough to make a moral revolution. He gets up early in the morning, just as our own aristocrats living the Simple Life get up early in the morning; because such altruism is much easier than stopping the games of the amphitheatre or giving the English people back their land. Marcus Aurelius is the most intolerable of human types. He is an unselfish egoist. An unselfish egoist is a man who has pride without the excuse of passion.

Of all conceivable forms of enlightenment the worst is what these people call the Inner Light. Of all horrible religions the most horrible is the worship of the god within. Any one who knows anybody knows how it would work; any one who knows any one from

---

[15] The "inner light" is the distinctive theme of the Society of Friends (Quakers), first expressed by George Fox in the 1600s, as he spoke of an individual's direct awareness of God and his will.

[16] Marcus Aurelius was the Roman emperor from AD 161 to 180. He was also a Stoic philosopher who believed the path to happiness is in accepting the present moment as it is, not being controlled by the desire for pleasure or fear of pain.

the Higher Thought Centre knows how it does work. That Jones shall worship the god within him turns out ultimately to mean that Jones shall worship Jones. Let Jones worship the sun or moon, anything rather than the Inner Light; let Jones worship cats or crocodiles, if he can find any in his street, but not the god within.

Christianity came into the world firstly in order to assert with violence that a man had not only to look inwards, but to look outwards, to behold with astonishment and enthusiasm a divine company and a divine captain. The only fun of being a Christian was that a man was not left alone with the Inner Light, but definitely recognized an outer light, fair as the sun, clear as the moon, terrible as an army with banners.

Christianity against Nature Worship

All the same, it will be as well if Jones does not worship the sun and moon. If he does, there is a tendency for him to imitate them; to say, that because the sun burns insects alive, he may burn insects alive. He thinks that because the sun gives people sun-stroke, he may give his neighbour measles. He thinks that because the moon is said to drive men mad, he may drive his wife mad.

This ugly side of mere external optimism had also shown itself in the ancient world. About the time when the Stoic idealism had begun to show the weaknesses of pessimism, the old nature worship of the ancients had begun to show the enormous weaknesses of optimism. Nature worship is natural enough while the society is young, or, in other words, Pantheism is all right as long as it is the worship of Pan.[17] But Nature has another side which experience and sin are not slow in finding out, and it is no flippancy to say of the god Pan that he soon showed the cloven hoof. The only objection to Natural Religion is that somehow it always becomes

[17] Pantheism refers to the belief that all things are divine, part of an all-encompassing, pervasive god. In Greek mythology Pan is the god of the wild, with hindquarters, legs, and horns of a goat (similar to a faun or satyr).

unnatural. A man loves Nature in the morning for her innocence and amiability, and at nightfall, if he is loving her still, it is for her darkness and her cruelty. He washes at dawn in clear water as did the Wise Man of the Stoics, yet, somehow at the dark end of the day, he is bathing in hot bull's blood, as did Julian the Apostate.[18]

The mere pursuit of health always leads to something unhealthy. Physical nature must not be made the direct object of obedience; it must be enjoyed, not worshipped. Stars and mountains must not be taken seriously. If they are, we end where the pagan nature worship ended. Because the earth is kind, we can imitate all her cruelties. Because sexuality is sane, we can all go mad about sexuality. Mere optimism had reached its insane and appropriate termination. The theory that everything was good had become an orgy of everything that was bad.

On the other side our idealist pessimists were represented by the old remnant of the Stoics. Marcus Aurelius and his friends had really given up the idea of any god in the universe and looked only to the god within. They had no hope of any virtue in nature, and hardly any hope of any virtue in society. They had not enough interest in the outer world really to wreck or revolutionise it. They did not love the city enough to set fire to it.

Thus the ancient world was exactly in our own desolate dilemma. The only people who really enjoyed this world were busy breaking it up; and the virtuous people did not care enough about them to knock them down.

Christianity's Dividing God from the Cosmos

In this dilemma (the same as ours) Christianity suddenly stepped in and offered a singular answer, which the world eventually accepted as *the* answer. It was the answer then, and I think it is the answer now.

---

[18] Julian was the Roman emperor from AD 361 to 363, best known for his rejection of Christianity.

This answer was like the slash of a sword; it sundered; it did not in any sense sentimentally unite. Briefly, it divided God from the cosmos. That transcendence and distinctness of the deity which some Christians now want to remove from Christianity, was really the only reason why any one wanted to be a Christian. It was the whole point of the Christian answer to the unhappy pessimist and the still more unhappy optimist.

As I am here only concerned with their particular problem, I shall indicate only briefly this great metaphysical suggestion. All descriptions of the creating or sustaining principle in things must be metaphorical, because they must be verbal. Thus the pantheist is forced to speak of God in all things as if he were in a box. Thus the evolutionist has, in his very name, the idea of being unrolled like a carpet. All terms, religious and irreligious, are open to this charge. The only question is whether all terms are useless, or whether one can, with such a phrase, cover a distinct *idea* about the origin of things. I think one can, and so evidently does the evolutionist, or he would not talk about evolution.

And the root phrase for all Christian theism was this, that God was a creator, as an artist is a creator. A poet is so separate from his poem that he himself speaks of it as a little thing he has "thrown off." Even in giving it forth he has flung it away. This principle that all creation and procreation is a breaking off is at least as consistent through the cosmos as the evolutionary principle that all growth is a branching out. A woman loses a child even in having a child. All creation is separation. Birth is as solemn a parting as death.

It was the prime philosophic principle of Christianity that this divorce in the divine act of making (such as severs the poet from the poem or the mother from the newborn child) was the true description of the act whereby the absolute energy made the world. According to most philosophers, God in making the world enslaved it. According to Christianity, in making it, He set it free. God had written, not so much a poem, but rather a play; a play he had planned as perfect, but which had necessarily been left to human actors and stage-managers, who had since made a great mess of it.

I will discuss the truth of this theorem later. Here I have only to point out with what a startling smoothness it passed the dilemma we have discussed in this chapter. In this way at least one could be both happy and indignant without degrading one's self to be either a pessimist or an optimist. On this system one could fight all the forces of existence without deserting the flag of existence. One could be at peace with the universe and yet be at war with the world. St. George could still fight the dragon, however big the monster bulked in the cosmos, though he were bigger than the mighty cities or bigger than the everlasting hills.[19] If he were as big as the world he could yet be killed in the name of the world. St. George had not to consider any obvious odds or proportions in the scale of things, but only the original secret of their design. He can shake his sword at the dragon, even if it is everything; even if the empty heavens over his head are only the huge arch of its open jaws.

Christianity as the Key that Fits

And then followed an experience impossible to describe. It was as if I had been blundering about since my birth with two huge and unmanageable machines, of different shapes and without apparent connection—the world and the Christian tradition. I had found this hole in the world: the fact that one must somehow find a way of loving the world without trusting it; somehow one must love the world without being worldly. I found this projecting feature of Christian theology, like a sort of hard spike, the dogmatic insistence that God was personal, and had made a world separate from Himself. The spike of dogma fitted exactly into the hole in the world—it had evidently been meant to go there—and then the strange thing began

---

[19] The legend of St. George and the Dragon tells of St. George taming and slaying a dragon in order to rescue a princess who was to be the dragon's next human sacrifice.

to happen. When once these two parts of the two machines had come together, one after another, all the other parts fitted and fell in with an eerie exactitude. I could hear bolt after bolt over all the machinery falling into its place with a kind of click of relief. Having got one part right, all the other parts were repeating that rectitude, as clock after clock strikes noon. Instinct after instinct was answered by doctrine after doctrine.

Or, to vary the metaphor, I was like one who had advanced into a hostile country to take one high fortress. And when that fort had fallen the whole country surrendered and turned solid behind me. The whole land was lit up, as it were, back to the first fields of my childhood. All those blind fancies of boyhood which in the fourth chapter I have tried in vain to trace on the darkness, became suddenly transparent and sane.

I was right when I felt that roses were red by some sort of choice: it was the divine choice.

I was right when I felt that I would almost rather say that grass was the wrong colour than say it must by necessity have been that colour: it might verily have been any other.

My sense that happiness hung on the crazy thread of a condition did mean something when all was said: it meant the whole doctrine of the Fall.

Even those dim and shapeless monsters of notions which I have not been able to describe, much less defend, stepped quietly into their places like colossal caryatides of the creed.[20]

The fancy that the cosmos was not vast and void, but small and cosy, had a fulfilled significance now, for anything that is a work of art must be small in the sight of the artist; to God the stars might be only small and dear, like diamonds.

And my haunting instinct that somehow good was not merely a tool to be used, but a relic to be guarded, like the goods from Crusoe's ship—even that had been the wild whisper of something

---

[20] A caryatides is a stone carving of a draped female figure, used as a pillar to support a Greek-style building.

originally wise, for, according to Christianity, we were indeed the survivors of a wreck, the crew of a golden ship that had gone down before the beginning of the world.

But the important matter was this, that it entirely reversed the reason for optimism. And the instant the reversal was made it felt like the abrupt ease when a bone is put back in the socket. I had often called myself an optimist, to avoid the too evident blasphemy of pessimism. But all the optimism of the age had been false and disheartening for this reason, that it had always been trying to prove that we fit in to the world. The Christian optimism is based on the fact that we do *not* fit in to the world.

I had tried to be happy by telling myself that man is an animal, like any other which sought its meat from God. But now I really was happy, for I had learnt that man is a monstrosity. I had been right in feeling all things as odd, for I myself was at once worse and better than all things. The optimist's pleasure was prosaic, for it dwelt on the naturalness of everything; the Christian pleasure was poetic, for it dwelt on the unnaturalness of everything in the light of the supernatural.

The modern philosopher had told me again and again that I was in the right place, and I had still felt depressed even in acquiescence. But I had heard that I was in the *wrong* place, and my soul sang for joy, like a bird in spring. The knowledge found out and illuminated forgotten chambers in the dark house of infancy. I knew now why grass had always seemed to me as queer as the green beard of a giant, and why I could feel homesick at home.

Chapter Summary

Chesterton began this chapter by contrasting the optimist and the pessimist's view of the world. Why do some people see nothing purposeful or meaningful in the world at all, while others love the world to the point they will defend the indefensible? Chesterton recognized that we belong to the world before we ask if it is nice to belong here. If we approach the world with the gratitude Chesterton wrote about in the previous chapter, then we will feel a cosmic loyalty to the world and realize that life is better than death, that existence is better than nonexistence. Why though do we still feel this tension of hating and loving the world? Isn't it true that reform is only possible when we hate something enough to change it, but also love it enough to think it worth changing?

Chesterton began to notice how Christianity had been accused of this very paradox—of believing the world is good *and* fallen, of being optimistic *and* pessimistic (in their glorious extremes, not a watered-down mixture) at the same time. He examined Christianity's radically different approaches to suicide versus martyrdom and then observed its ability to avoid worshipping both the god within (Inner Light) and the god without (nature worship). By dividing God from the cosmos, both truths come into focus: the world is the good creation of a personal God and the world is fallen and not as it should be. This was the key that opened Chesterton up to the rest of Christianity and explained how it was possible for him to "feel homesick at home."

Discussion Questions

1. Why do you think Chesterton named this chapter "The Flag of the World"?
2. What do you think of how Chesterton describes the right kind of patriotism?

3. What are the dangers of worshipping the god within (Inner Light)? What about worshipping the god without (nature worship)?
4. What are some evidences of the world's goodness? What about its fallenness?

SIX

In the previous chapter Chesterton explained what it was like when he suddenly saw how the Christian view of the world was a key that fits into a lock. In this chapter he takes his argument a step further, watching how the peculiarities of Christian doctrine are strange or "go wrong" in precisely the way the world itself is strange or goes wrong. Chesterton claims it was not the Christian apologist who convinced him of the Christian creed, but the inconsistent and contradictory reasons the critics of Christianity gave for rejecting it. This chapter, with its focus on paradox, is the key to *Orthodoxy* and, in some ways, to Chesterton's thinking overall.

Chesterton's goal in this chapter is to turn the tables on those who say the Christian creed is too simple. It is complex, he says, because truth is complex. Chesterton draws attention to the inconsistency of the critics of Christianity in order to make the case that if these contradictory criticisms were all somehow true, then Christianity is either the worst blight on humanity or the right key to understanding life and the world. He argues that paradox is the key to ethics—Christianity allows for the collision of "passions apparently opposite." He also defends the church's preoccupation with getting doctrine right even in the smallest details because precision matters if you are to maintain your balance.

Memorable Parts to Look For

- The contradictory nature of criticisms launched against Christianity
- Chesterton's description of courage
- The illustration of Christianity as "a huge and ragged and romantic rock"
- The thrilling romance of orthodoxy in avoiding traps on every side

The Paradoxes of Christianity

The real trouble with this world of ours is not that it is an unreasonable world, nor even that it is a reasonable one. The commonest kind of trouble is that it is nearly reasonable, but not quite. Life is not an illogicality; yet it is a trap for logicians. It looks just a little more mathematical and regular than it is; its exactitude is obvious, but its inexactitude is hidden; its wildness lies in wait.

I give one coarse instance of what I mean. Suppose some mathematical creature from the moon were to reckon up the human body; he would at once see that the essential thing about it was that it was duplicate. A man is two men, he on the right exactly resembling him on the left. Having noted that there was an arm on the right and one on the left, a leg on the right and one on the left, he might go further and still find on each side the same number of fingers, the same number of toes, twin eyes, twin ears, twin nostrils, and even twin lobes of the brain. At last he would take it as a law; and then, where he found a heart on one side, would deduce that there was another heart on the other. And just then, where he most felt he was right, he would be wrong.

It is this silent swerving from accuracy by an inch that is the uncanny element in everything. It seems a sort of secret treason in the universe.

An apple or an orange is round enough to get itself called round, and yet is not round after all.

The earth itself is shaped like an orange in order to lure some simple astronomer into calling it a globe.

A blade of grass is called after the blade of a sword, because it comes to a point; but it doesn't.

Everywhere in things there is this element of the quiet and incalculable. It escapes the rationalists, but it never escapes till the last moment. From the grand curve of our earth it could easily be inferred that every inch of it was thus curved. It would seem rational that as a man has a brain on both sides, he should have a heart on both sides. Yet scientific men are still organizing expeditions to find the North Pole, because they are so fond of flat country. Scientific men are also still organizing expeditions to find a man's heart; and when they try to find it, they generally get on the wrong side of him.

Now, actual insight or inspiration is best tested by whether it guesses these hidden malformations or surprises. If our mathematician from the moon saw the two arms and the two ears, he might deduce the two shoulder blades and the two halves of the brain. But if he guessed that the man's heart was in the right place, then I should call him something more than a mathematician. Now, this is exactly the claim which I have since come to propound for Christianity. Not merely that it deduces logical truths, but that when it suddenly becomes illogical, it has found, so to speak, an illogical truth. It not only goes right about things, but it goes wrong (if one may say so) exactly where the things go wrong. Its plan suits the secret irregularities, and expects the unexpected. It is simple about the simple truth; but it is stubborn about the subtle truth. It will admit that a man has two hands, it will not admit (though all the Modernists wail to it) the obvious deduction that he has two hearts. It is my only purpose in this chapter to point this out; to show that whenever we feel there is something odd in Christian theology, we shall generally find that there is something odd in the truth.

The Complexity of the Christian Creed

I have alluded to an unmeaning phrase to the effect that such and such a creed cannot be believed in our age. Of course, anything can be believed in any age. But, oddly enough, there really is a sense in which a creed, if it is believed at all, can be believed more fixedly in a complex society than in a simple one. If a man finds Christianity true in Birmingham, he has actually clearer reasons for faith than if he had found it true in Mercia.[1] For the more complicated seems the coincidence, the less it can be a coincidence. If snowflakes fell in the shape, say, of the heart of Midlothian,[2] it might be an accident. But if snowflakes fell in the exact shape of the maze at Hampton Court,[3] I think one might call it a miracle.

It is exactly as of such a miracle that I have since come to feel of the philosophy of Christianity. The complication of our modern world proves the truth of the creed more perfectly than any of the plain problems of the ages of faith. It was in Notting Hill and Battersea that I began to see that Christianity was true.[4]

This is why the faith has that elaboration of doctrines and details which so much distresses those who admire Christianity without believing in it. When once one believes in a creed, one is proud of its complexity, as scientists are proud of the complexity of science. It shows how rich it is in discoveries. If it is right at all, it

---

[1] Birmingham is a city in England. Mercia was one of the Anglo-Saxon kingdoms in the Heptarchy, founded in the sixth century.

[2] The Heart of Midlothian is a heart-shaped mosaic, formed in colored granite setts, built into the pavement in the High Street section of the Royal Mile in Edinburgh.

[3] The UK's oldest surviving hedge maze, commissioned around the year 1700.

[4] Notting Hill is a district of west London. Battersea is a district of southwest London.

is a compliment to say that it's elaborately right. A stick might fit a hole or a stone a hollow by accident. But a key and a lock are both complex. And if a key fits a lock, you know it is the right key.

Christianity and the Accumulation of Truth

But this involved accuracy of the thing makes it very difficult to do what I now have to do, to describe this accumulation of truth. It is very hard for a man to defend anything of which he is entirely convinced. It is comparatively easy when he is only partially convinced. He is partially convinced because he has found this or that proof of the thing, and he can expound it. But a man is not really convinced of a philosophic theory when he finds that something proves it. He is only really convinced when he finds that everything proves it. And the more converging reasons he finds pointing to this conviction, the more bewildered he is if asked suddenly to sum them up.

Thus, if one asked an ordinary intelligent man, on the spur of the moment, "Why do you prefer civilization to savagery?" he would look wildly round at object after object, and would only be able to answer vaguely, "Why, there is that bookcase . . . and the coals in the coal-scuttle . . . and pianos . . . and policemen." The whole case for civilization is that the case for it is complex. It has done so many things. But that very multiplicity of proof which ought to make reply overwhelming makes reply impossible.

There is, therefore, about all complete conviction a kind of huge helplessness. The belief is so big that it takes a long time to get it into action. And this hesitation chiefly arises, oddly enough, from an indifference about where one should begin. All roads lead to Rome; which is one reason why many people never get there. In the case of this defence of the Christian conviction I confess that I would as soon begin the argument with one thing as another; I would begin it with a turnip or a taximeter cab. But if I am to be at all careful about making my meaning clear, it will, I think, be wiser to continue the current arguments of the last chapter, which was concerned to urge the first of these mystical coincidences, or rather ratifications.

The Contradictions of Christianity's Critics

All I had hitherto heard of Christian theology had alienated me from it. I was a pagan at the age of twelve, and a complete agnostic by the age of sixteen; and I cannot understand any one passing the age of seventeen without having asked himself so simple a question. I did, indeed, retain a cloudy reverence for a cosmic deity and a great historical interest in the Founder of Christianity. But I certainly regarded Him as a man; though perhaps I thought that, even in that point, He had an advantage over some of His modern critics.

I read the scientific and sceptical literature of my time—all of it, at least, that I could find written in English and lying about; and I read nothing else; I mean I read nothing else on any other note of philosophy. The penny dreadfuls which I also read were indeed in a healthy and heroic tradition of Christianity; but I did not know this at the time. I never read a line of Christian apologetics. I read as little as I can of them now. It was Huxley and Herbert Spencer and Bradlaugh who brought me back to orthodox theology.[5] They sowed in my mind my first wild doubts of doubt. Our grandmothers were quite right when they said that Tom Paine and the freethinkers unsettled the mind. They do.[6] They unsettled mine horribly. The rationalist made me question whether reason was of any use whatever; and when I had finished Herbert Spencer I had got as far as doubting (for the first time) whether evolution had occurred at all.

---

[5] Charles Bradlaugh (1833–91) was an English political activist and atheist, the founder of the National Secular Society in 1866.

[6] Thomas Paine (1737–1809), the American political activist and philosopher, authored the two most influential pamphlets at the start of the American Revolution. He was an advocate of free thought and the author of *The Rights of Man.*

As I laid down the last of Colonel Ingersoll's atheistic lectures,[7] the dreadful thought broke across my mind, "Almost thou persuadest me to be a Christian."[8] I was in a desperate way.

This odd effect of the great agnostics in arousing doubts deeper than their own might be illustrated in many ways. I take only one. As I read and re-read all the non-Christian or anti-Christian accounts of the faith, from Huxley to Bradlaugh, a slow and awful impression grew gradually but graphically upon my mind—the impression that Christianity must be a most extraordinary thing. For not only (as I understood) had Christianity the most flaming vices, but it had apparently a mystical talent for combining vices which seemed inconsistent with each other. It was attacked on all sides and for all contradictory reasons. No sooner had one rationalist demonstrated that it was too far to the east than another demonstrated with equal clearness that it was much too far to the west. No sooner had my indignation died down at its angular and aggressive squareness than I was called up again to notice and condemn its enervating and sensual roundness.

In case any reader has not come across the thing I mean, I will give such instances as I remember at random of this self-contradiction in the sceptical attack. I give four or five of them; there are fifty more.

Christianity Is Too Pessimistic and Too Optimistic

Thus, for instance, I was much moved by the eloquent attack on Christianity as a thing of inhuman gloom; for I thought (and still think) sincere pessimism the unpardonable sin. Insincere pessimism is a social accomplishment, rather agreeable than otherwise; and fortunately nearly all pessimism is insincere. But if Christianity

---

[7] Robert Ingersoll (1833–99) was an American writer who campaigned in defense of agnosticism.

[8] Acts 26:28: "Almost thou persuadest me to be a Christian" is King Agrippa's response to the apostle Paul's testimony.

was, as these people said, a thing purely pessimistic and opposed to life, then I was quite prepared to blow up St. Paul's Cathedral.

But the extraordinary thing is this. They did prove to me in Chapter I. (to my complete satisfaction) that Christianity was too pessimistic; and then, in Chapter II., they began to prove to me that it was a great deal too optimistic.

One accusation against Christianity was that it prevented men, by morbid tears and terrors, from seeking joy and liberty in the bosom of Nature. But another accusation was that it comforted men with a fictitious providence, and put them in a pink-and-white nursery.

One great agnostic asked why Nature was not beautiful enough, and why it was hard to be free. Another great agnostic objected that Christian optimism, "the garment of make-believe woven by pious hands," hid from us the fact that Nature was ugly, and that it was impossible to be free.

One rationalist had hardly done calling Christianity a nightmare before another began to call it a fool's paradise. This puzzled me; the charges seemed inconsistent. Christianity could not at once be the black mask on a white world, and also the white mask on a black world. The state of the Christian could not be at once so comfortable that he was a coward to cling to it, and so uncomfortable that he was a fool to stand it. If it falsified human vision it must falsify it one way or another; it could not wear both green and rose-coloured spectacles.

I rolled on my tongue with a terrible joy, as did all young men of that time, the taunts which Swinburne hurled at the dreariness of the creed—

> "Thou hast conquered, O pale Galilaean, the world has grown gray with Thy breath."[9]

---

[9] Chesterton is quoting here from the "Hymn to Proserpine," a poem published in 1866 by Algernon Charles Swinburne (1837–1909). The poem is addressed to the goddess Proserpina and laments the rise of Christianity for displacing the pagan goddess and her pantheon.

But when I read the same poet's accounts of paganism (as in "Atalanta"), I gathered that the world was, if possible, more gray before the Galilean breathed on it than afterwards. The poet maintained, indeed, in the abstract, that life itself was pitch dark. And yet, somehow, Christianity had darkened it. The very man who denounced Christianity for pessimism was himself a pessimist. I thought there must be something wrong. And it did for one wild moment cross my mind that, perhaps, those might not be the very best judges of the relation of religion to happiness who, by their own account, had neither one nor the other.

It must be understood that I did not conclude hastily that the accusations were false or the accusers fools. I simply deduced that Christianity must be something even weirder and wickeder than they made out. A thing might have these two opposite vices; but it must be a rather queer thing if it did. A man might be too fat in one place and too thin in another; but he would be an odd shape. At this point my thoughts were only of the odd shape of the Christian religion; I did not allege any odd shape in the rationalistic mind.

Christianity Is Too Weak and Too Warlike

Here is another case of the same kind. I felt that a strong case against Christianity lay in the charge that there is something timid, monkish, and unmanly about all that is called "Christian," especially in its attitude towards resistance and fighting. The great sceptics of the nineteenth century were largely virile. Bradlaugh in an expansive way, Huxley, in a reticent way, were decidedly men. In comparison, it did seem tenable that there was something weak and over patient about Christian counsels. The Gospel paradox about the other cheek,[10] the fact that priests never fought, a hundred things

[10] In the Sermon on the Mount, Jesus commanded his followers, "That ye resist not evil: but whosoever shall smite thee on thy right cheek, turn to him the other also" (Matt 5:39).

made plausible the accusation that Christianity was an attempt to make a man too like a sheep. I read it and believed it, and if I had read nothing different, I should have gone on believing it.

But I read something very different. I turned the next page in my agnostic manual, and my brain turned upside down. Now I found that I was to hate Christianity not for fighting too little, but for fighting too much. Christianity, it seemed, was the mother of wars. Christianity had deluged the world with blood. I had got thoroughly angry with the Christian, because he never was angry. And now I was told to be angry with him because his anger had been the most huge and horrible thing in human history; because his anger had soaked the earth and smoked to the sun.

The very people who reproached Christianity with the meekness and non-resistance of the monasteries were the very people who reproached it also with the violence and valour of the Crusades. It was the fault of poor old Christianity (somehow or other) both that Edward the Confessor did not fight and that Richard Coeur de Leon did.[11] The Quakers (we were told) were the only characteristic Christians; and yet the massacres of Cromwell and Alva were characteristic Christian crimes.[12]

What could it all mean? What was this Christianity which always forbade war and always produced wars? What could be the nature of the thing which one could abuse first because it would not fight, and second because it was always fighting? In what world of riddles

[11] Edward the Confessor (1003–66) was among the last Anglo-Saxon kings of England. He reigned from 1042 to 1066. He was the first king buried in Westminster Abbey. Richard I (also known as Richard the Lionheart) (1157–99) was king of England from 1189 to 1199 and was known for being a great military leader and warrior.

[12] Oliver Cromwell (1599–1658) was an English general who led the Parliament's armies against King Charles I during the English Civil War. Many historians believe him to have been responsible for the killing of thousands of civilians in Ireland. The Duke of Alva (1508–82) opposed the rebels against Spain in the Netherlands and is said to have been responsible for the execution of thousands of people.

was born this monstrous murder and this monstrous meekness? The shape of Christianity grew a queerer shape every instant.

Christianity's Creed Divides and Unites

I take a third case; the strangest of all, because it involves the one real objection to the faith. The one real objection to the Christian religion is simply that it is one religion. The world is a big place, full of very different kinds of people. Christianity (it may reasonably be said) is one thing confined to one kind of people; it began in Palestine, it has practically stopped with Europe.

I was duly impressed with this argument in my youth, and I was much drawn towards the doctrine often preached in Ethical Societies—I mean the doctrine that there is one great unconscious church of all humanity founded on the omnipresence of the human conscience. Creeds, it was said, divided men; but at least morals united them. The soul might seek the strangest and most remote lands and ages and still find essential ethical common sense. It might find Confucius under Eastern trees,[13] and he would be writing "Thou shalt not steal." It might decipher the darkest hieroglyphic on the most primeval desert, and the meaning when deciphered would be "Little boys should tell the truth."

I believed this doctrine of the brotherhood of all men in the possession of a moral sense, and I believe it still—with other things. And I was thoroughly annoyed with Christianity for suggesting (as I supposed) that whole ages and empires of men had utterly escaped this light of justice and reason.

But then I found an astonishing thing. I found that the very people who said that mankind was one church from Plato to Emerson were the very people who said that morality had changed altogether,

---

[13] Confucius (551–479 BC) was a Chinese philosopher whose followers emphasized personal and governmental morality, correctness of social relationships, justice, kindness, and sincerity.

and that what was right in one age was wrong in another.[14] If I asked, say, for an altar, I was told that we needed none, for men our brothers gave us clear oracles and one creed in their universal customs and ideals. But if I mildly pointed out that one of men's universal customs was to have an altar, then my agnostic teachers turned clean round and told me that men had always been in darkness and the superstitions of savages. I found it was their daily taunt against Christianity that it was the light of one people and had left all others to die in the dark. But I also found that it was their special boast for themselves that science and progress were the discovery of one people, and that all other peoples had died in the dark. Their chief insult to Christianity was actually their chief compliment to themselves, and there seemed to be a strange unfairness about all their relative insistence on the two things.

When considering some pagan or agnostic, we were to remember that all men had one religion; when considering some mystic or spiritualist, we were only to consider what absurd religions some men had. We could trust the ethics of Epictetus,[15] because ethics had never changed. We must not trust the ethics of Bossuet,[16] because ethics had changed. They changed in two hundred years, but not in two thousand.

This began to be alarming. It looked not so much as if Christianity was bad enough to include any vices, but rather as if any stick was good enough to beat Christianity with. What again could this astonishing thing be like which people were so anxious to contradict, that in doing so they did not mind contradicting themselves? I saw the same thing on every side.

---

[14] Ralph Waldo Emerson (1803–82) was an American essayist and poet whose philosophical work led the transcendentalist movement of the mid-nineteenth century.

[15] Epictetus was a Greek Stoic philosopher (AD 50–135).

[16] Jacques Bossuet (1627–1704) was a French bishop and theologian best known for his oratorical skills.

Other Accusations against Christianity

I can give no further space to this discussion of it in detail; but lest any one supposes that I have unfairly selected three accidental cases I will run briefly through a few others.

Thus, certain sceptics wrote that the great crime of Christianity had been its attack on the family; it had dragged women to the loneliness and contemplation of the cloister, away from their homes and their children. But, then, other sceptics (slightly more advanced) said that the great crime of Christianity was forcing the family and marriage upon us; that it doomed women to the drudgery of their homes and children, and forbade them loneliness and contemplation. The charge was actually reversed.

Or, again, certain phrases in the Epistles or the marriage service, were said by the anti-Christians to show contempt for woman's intellect. But I found that the anti-Christians themselves had a contempt for woman's intellect; for it was their great sneer at the Church on the Continent that "only women" went to it.

Or again, Christianity was reproached with its naked and hungry habits; with its sackcloth and dried peas. But the next minute Christianity was being reproached with its pomp and its ritualism; its shrines of porphyry and its robes of gold. It was abused for being too plain and for being too coloured.

Again Christianity had always been accused of restraining sexuality too much, when Bradlaugh the Malthusian discovered that it restrained it too little.[17]

It is often accused in the same breath of prim respectability and of religious extravagance.

Between the covers of the same atheistic pamphlet I have found the faith rebuked for its disunion, "One thinks one thing, and one

---

[17] Charles Bradlaugh supported Malthusian theories, named after Thomas Robert Malthus (1766–1834), about curbing population growth.

another," and rebuked also for its union, "It is difference of opinion that prevents the world from going to the dogs."

In the same conversation a freethinker, a friend of mine, blamed Christianity for despising Jews, and then despised it himself for being Jewish.

Weighing the Nature of These Accusations

I wished to be quite fair then, and I wish to be quite fair now; and I did not conclude that the attack on Christianity was all wrong. I only concluded that if Christianity was wrong, it was very wrong indeed. Such hostile horrors might be combined in one thing, but that thing must be very strange and solitary. There are men who are misers, and also spendthrifts; but they are rare. There are men sensual and also ascetic; but they are rare.

But if this mass of mad contradictions really existed, quakerish and bloodthirsty, too gorgeous and too thread-bare, austere, yet pandering preposterously to the lust of the eye, the enemy of women and their foolish refuge, a solemn pessimist and a silly optimist, if this evil existed, then there was in this evil something quite supreme and unique. For I found in my rationalist teachers no explanation of such exceptional corruption. Christianity (theoretically speaking) was in their eyes only one of the ordinary myths and errors of mortals. *They* gave me no key to this twisted and unnatural badness. Such a paradox of evil rose to the stature of the supernatural. It was, indeed, almost as supernatural as the infallibility of the Pope.

An historic institution, which never went right, is really quite as much of a miracle as an institution that cannot go wrong. The only explanation which immediately occurred to my mind was that Christianity did not come from heaven, but from hell. Really, if Jesus of Nazareth was not Christ, He must have been Antichrist.

The Thunderbolt: Christianity as the Centre

And then in a quiet hour a strange thought struck me like a still thunderbolt. There had suddenly come into my mind another explanation.

Suppose we heard an unknown man spoken of by many men. Suppose we were puzzled to hear that some men said he was too tall and some too short; some objected to his fatness, some lamented his leanness; some thought him too dark, and some too fair.

One explanation (as has been already admitted) would be that he might be an odd shape. But there is another explanation. He might be the right shape.

Outrageously tall men might feel him to be short. Very short men might feel him to be tall. Old bucks who are growing stout might consider him insufficiently filled out; old beaux who were growing thin might feel that he expanded beyond the narrow lines of elegance. Perhaps Swedes (who have pale hair like tow) called him a dark man, while negroes considered him distinctly blonde. Perhaps (in short) this extraordinary thing is really the ordinary thing; at least the normal thing, the centre.

Perhaps, after all, it is Christianity that is sane and all its critics that are mad—in various ways. I tested this idea by asking myself whether there was about any of the accusers anything morbid that might explain the accusation. I was startled to find that this key fitted a lock.

For instance, it was certainly odd that the modern world charged Christianity at once with bodily austerity and with artistic pomp. But then it was also odd, very odd, that the modern world itself combined extreme bodily luxury with an extreme absence of artistic pomp. The modern man thought Becket's robes too rich and his meals too poor.[18] But then the modern man was really exceptional in history; no man before ever ate such elaborate dinners in such

---

[18] Thomas Becket (1118–70) was archbishop of Canterbury from 1162 to 1170.

ugly clothes. The modern man found the church too simple exactly where modern life is too complex; he found the church too gorgeous exactly where modern life is too dingy. The man who disliked the plain fasts and feasts was mad on entrees. The man who disliked vestments wore a pair of preposterous trousers. And surely if there was any insanity involved in the matter at all it was in the trousers, not in the simply falling robe. If there was any insanity at all, it was in the extravagant entrees, not in the bread and wine.

I went over all the cases, and I found the key fitted so far. The fact that Swinburne was irritated at the unhappiness of Christians and yet more irritated at their happiness was easily explained. It was no longer a complication of diseases in Christianity, but a complication of diseases in Swinburne. The restraints of Christians saddened him simply because he was more hedonist than a healthy man should be. The faith of Christians angered him because he was more pessimist than a healthy man should be.

In the same way the Malthusians by instinct attacked Christianity; not because there is anything especially anti-Malthusian about Christianity, but because there is something a little anti-human about Malthusianism.

Christianity's Paradoxical Sanity

Nevertheless it could not, I felt, be quite true that Christianity was merely sensible and stood in the middle. There was really an element in it of emphasis and even frenzy which had justified the secularists in their superficial criticism. It might be wise, I began more and more to think that it was wise, but it was not merely worldly wise; it was not merely temperate and respectable. Its fierce crusaders and meek saints might balance each other; still, the crusaders were very fierce and the saints were very meek, meek beyond all decency.

Now, it was just at this point of the speculation that I remembered my thoughts about the martyr and the suicide. In that matter there had been this combination between two almost insane positions which yet somehow amounted to sanity. This was just such another contradiction; and this I had already found to be true. This was exactly one of the paradoxes in which sceptics found the creed wrong; and in this I had found it right. Madly as Christians might love the martyr or hate the suicide, they never felt these passions more madly than I had felt them long before I dreamed of Christianity.

Then the most difficult and interesting part of the mental process opened, and I began to trace this idea darkly through all the enormous thoughts of our theology. The idea was that which I had outlined touching the optimist and the pessimist; that we want not an amalgam or compromise, but both things at the top of their energy; love and wrath both burning. Here I shall only trace it in relation to ethics. But I need not remind the reader that the idea of this combination is indeed central in orthodox theology. For orthodox theology has specially insisted that Christ was not a being apart from God and man, like an elf, nor yet a being half human and half not, like a centaur, but both things at once and both things thoroughly, very man and very God. Now let me trace this notion as I found it.

Christianity as a Collision of Passions

All sane men can see that sanity is some kind of equilibrium; that one may be mad and eat too much, or mad and eat too little. Some moderns have indeed appeared with vague versions of progress and evolution which seeks to destroy the *meson* or balance of Aristotle.[19] They seem to suggest that we are meant to starve progressively, or to go on eating larger and larger breakfasts every morning forever. But the great truism of the *meson* remains for all thinking men,

---

[19] In book 2 of *Nicomachean Ethics,* Aristotle describes a view of virtue known as the "Doctrine of the Mean" (or *meson*), in which virtuous character is exhibited through maintaining a balance between two correlative vices (which are usually a deficiency or excess of a virtuous characteristic).

and these people have not upset any balance except their own. But granted that we have all to keep a balance, the real interest comes in with the question of how that balance can be kept. That was the problem which Paganism tried to solve: that was the problem which I think Christianity solved and solved in a very strange way.

Paganism declared that virtue was in a balance; Christianity declared it was in a conflict: the collision of two passions apparently opposite. Of course they were not really inconsistent; but they were such that it was hard to hold simultaneously.

An Example: Courage

Let us follow for a moment the clue of the martyr and the suicide; and take the case of courage. No quality has ever so much addled the brains and tangled the definitions of merely rational sages. Courage is almost a contradiction in terms. It means a strong desire to live taking the form of a readiness to die. "He that will lose his life, the same shall save it,"[20] is not a piece of mysticism for saints and heroes. It is a piece of everyday advice for sailors or mountaineers. It might be printed in an Alpine guide or a drill book. This paradox is the whole principle of courage; even of quite earthly or quite brutal courage. A man cut off by the sea may save his life if he will risk it on the precipice. He can only get away from death by continually stepping within an inch of it. A soldier surrounded by enemies, if he is to cut his way out, needs to combine a strong desire for living with a strange carelessness about dying. He must not merely cling to life, for then he will be a coward, and will not escape. He must not merely wait for death, for then he will be a suicide, and will not escape. He must seek his life in a spirit of furious indifference to it; he must desire life like water and yet drink death like wine.

No philosopher, I fancy, has ever expressed this romantic riddle with adequate lucidity, and I certainly have not done so. But Christianity has done more: it has marked the limits of it in the

---

[20] Chesterton's rendering of Jesus's words in Matt 16:25.

awful graves of the suicide and the hero, showing the distance between him who dies for the sake of living and him who dies for the sake of dying. And it has held up ever since above the European lances the banner of the mystery of chivalry: the Christian courage, which is a disdain of death; not the Chinese courage, which is a disdain of life.

And now I began to find that this duplex passion was the Christian key to ethics everywhere. Everywhere the creed made a moderation out of the still crash of two impetuous emotions.

Another Example: Humility

Take, for instance, the matter of modesty, of the balance between mere pride and mere prostration. The average pagan, like the average agnostic, would merely say that he was content with himself, but not insolently self-satisfied, that there were many better and many worse, that his deserts were limited, but he would see that he got them. In short, he would walk with his head in the air; but not necessarily with his nose in the air.

This is a manly and rational position, but it is open to the objection we noted against the compromise between optimism and pessimism—the "resignation" of Matthew Arnold. Being a mixture of two things, it is a dilution of two things; neither is present in its full strength or contributes its full colour. This proper pride does not lift the heart like the tongue of trumpets; you cannot go clad in crimson and gold for this.

On the other hand, this mild rationalist modesty does not cleanse the soul with fire and make it clear like crystal; it does not (like a strict and searching humility) make a man as a little child, who can sit at the feet of the grass. It does not make him look up and see marvels; for Alice must grow small if she is to be *Alice in Wonderland*.[21] Thus it loses both the poetry of being proud and the poetry of being humble.

---

[21] *Alice's Adventures in Wonderland* by Lewis Carroll, published in 1865.

Christianity sought by this same strange expedient to save both of them. It separated the two ideas and then exaggerated them both. In one way Man was to be haughtier than he had ever been before; in another way he was to be humbler than he had ever been before. Insofar as I am Man I am the chief of creatures. Insofar as I am a man I am the chief of sinners.

All humility that had meant pessimism, that had meant man taking a vague or mean view of his whole destiny—all that was to go. We were to hear no more the wail of Ecclesiastes that humanity had no pre-eminence over the brute,[22] or the awful cry of Homer that man was only the saddest of all the beasts of the field. Man was a statue of God walking about the garden. Man had pre-eminence over all the brutes; man was only sad because he was not a beast, but a broken god. The Greek had spoken of men creeping on the earth, as if clinging to it. Now Man was to tread on the earth as if to subdue it.

Christianity thus held a thought of the dignity of man that could only be expressed in crowns rayed like the sun and fans of peacock plumage. Yet at the same time it could hold a thought about the abject smallness of man that could only be expressed in fasting and fantastic submission, in the gray ashes of St. Dominic and the white snows of St. Bernard.[23] When one came to think of *one's self*, there was vista and void enough for any amount of bleak abnegation and bitter truth. There the realistic gentleman could let himself go—as long as he let himself go at himself.

There was an open playground for the happy pessimist. Let him say anything against himself short of blaspheming the original aim of his being; let him call himself a fool and even a damned fool

[22] Ecclesiastes is one of the books of wisdom in the Old Testament, traditionally attributed to King Solomon.

[23] Saint Dominic (1170–1221) was a Castilian priest and founder of the Dominican Order. Saint Bernard of Menthon (1020–81) was an Italian monk who founded a hospice and monastery in one of the coldest and most treacherous parts of the Western Alps.

(though that is Calvinistic); but he must not say that fools are not worth saving. He must not say that a man, *qua* man, can be valueless. Here, again in short, Christianity got over the difficulty of combining furious opposites, by keeping them both, and keeping them both furious. The Church was positive on both points. One can hardly think too little of one's self. One can hardly think too much of one's soul.

Another Example: Charity

Take another case: the complicated question of charity, which some highly uncharitable idealists seem to think quite easy. Charity is a paradox, like modesty and courage. Stated baldly, charity certainly means one of two things—pardoning unpardonable acts, or loving unlovable people.

But if we ask ourselves (as we did in the case of pride) what a sensible pagan would feel about such a subject, we shall probably be beginning at the bottom of it. A sensible pagan would say that there were some people one could forgive, and someone couldn't: a slave who stole wine could be laughed at; a slave who betrayed his benefactor could be killed, and cursed even after he was killed. Insofar as the act was pardonable, the man was pardonable. That again is rational, and even refreshing; but it is a dilution. It leaves no place for a pure horror of injustice, such as that which is a great beauty in the innocent. And it leaves no place for a mere tenderness for men as men, such as is the whole fascination of the charitable.

Christianity came in here as before. It came in startlingly with a sword, and clove one thing from another. It divided the crime from the criminal. The criminal we must forgive unto seventy times seven.[24] The crime we must not forgive at all. It was not enough that slaves who stole wine inspired partly anger and partly kindness. We must be much more angry with theft than before, and yet much kinder to thieves than before. There was room for wrath and love to

[24] Jesus's admonition to Peter in Matt 18:21–22.

run wild. And the more I considered Christianity, the more I found that while it had established a rule and order, the chief aim of that order was to give room for good things to run wild.

Freedom and the Paradoxes of Christianity

Mental and emotional liberty are not so simple as they look. Really they require almost as careful a balance of laws and conditions as do social and political liberty. The ordinary aesthetic anarchist who sets out to feel everything freely gets knotted at last in a paradox that prevents him feeling at all. He breaks away from home limits to follow poetry. But in ceasing to feel home limits he has ceased to feel the "Odyssey."[25] He is free from national prejudices and outside patriotism. But being outside patriotism he is outside "Henry V."[26] Such a literary man is simply outside all literature: he is more of a prisoner than any bigot. For if there is a wall between you and the world, it makes little difference whether you describe yourself as locked in or as locked out.

What we want is not the universality that is outside all normal sentiments; we want the universality that is inside all normal sentiments. It is all the difference between being free from them, as a man is free from a prison, and being free of them as a man is free of a city. I am free from Windsor Castle (that is, I am not forcibly detained there),[27] but I am by no means free of that building. How can man be approximately free of fine emotions, able to swing them in a clear space without breakage or wrong? *This* was the achievement of this Christian paradox of the parallel passions. Granted the primary dogma of the war between divine and diabolic, the revolt and ruin of the world, their optimism and pessimism, as pure poetry, could be loosened like cataracts.

---

[25] *The Odyssey* is Homer's epic of Odysseus's ten-year struggle to return home after the Trojan War.

[26] *Henry V* is a history play by William Shakespeare.

[27] Windsor Castle is a royal residence in the English county of Berkshire.

St. Francis, in praising all good, could be a more shouting optimist than Walt Whitman.[28] St. Jerome, in denouncing all evil, could paint the world blacker than Schopenhauer.[29] Both passions were free because both were kept in their place.

The optimist could pour out all the praise he liked on the gay music of the march, the golden trumpets, and the purple banners going into battle. But he must not call the fight needless. The pessimist might draw as darkly as he chose the sickening marches or the sanguine wounds. But he must not call the fight hopeless. So it was with all the other moral problems, with pride, with protest, and with compassion.

By defining its main doctrine, the Church not only kept seemingly inconsistent things side by side, but, what was more, allowed them to break out in a sort of artistic violence otherwise possible only to anarchists. Meekness grew more dramatic than madness. Historic Christianity rose into a high and strange *coup de theatre* of morality—things that are to virtue what the crimes of Nero are to vice.[30] The spirits of indignation and of charity took terrible and attractive forms, ranging from that monkish fierceness that scourged like a dog the first and greatest of the Plantagenets,[31] to the sublime pity of St. Catherine, who, in the official shambles,

---

[28] Francis of Assisi (1181–1226) was an Italian Catholic friar, deacon, and preacher, known for his founding of the Franciscan Orders and embrace of the goodness of creation. Chesterton wrote a book on Saint Francis in 1923. Walt Whitman (1819–92) was an American poet, essayist, and journalist, known as the father of free verse.

[29] Jerome (347–420) was an influential theologian and translator of the Latin Vulgate. Arthur Schopenhauer (1788–1860) was a German philosopher best known for his work characterizing the world as the product of a blind and insatiable metaphysical will.

[30] A *coup de theatre* is a dramatically sudden turn of events, usually in a play. Nero, notorious for his paranoia and his crimes against Christians, was Roman emperor from AD 54 to 68.

[31] The Plantagenets were a powerful family in Europe. Henry II (1133–89) is considered the first Plantagenet king of England. Here Chesterton is referring to his public penance after the murder of Thomas Becket.

kissed the bloody head of the criminal.[32] Poetry could be acted as well as composed.

This heroic and monumental manner in ethics has entirely vanished with supernatural religion. They, being humble, could parade themselves: but we are too proud to be prominent. Our ethical teachers write reasonably for prison reform; but we are not likely to see Mr. Cadbury,[33] or any eminent philanthropist, go into Reading Gaol and embrace the strangled corpse before it is cast into the quicklime. Our ethical teachers write mildly against the power of millionaires; but we are not likely to see Mr. Rockefeller,[34] or any modern tyrant, publicly whipped in Westminster Abbey.

Christian Virtues Side by Side

Thus, the double charges of the secularists, though throwing nothing but darkness and confusion on themselves, throw a real light on the faith. It is true that the historic Church has at once emphasised celibacy and emphasised the family; has at once (if one may put it so) been fiercely for having children and fiercely for not having children. It has kept them side by side like two strong colours, red and white, like the red and white upon the shield of St. George. It has always had a healthy hatred of pink. It hates that combination of two colours which is the feeble expedient of the philosophers. It hates that evolution of black into white which is tantamount to a dirty gray. In fact, the whole theory of the Church on virginity

[32] Catherine of Siena (1347–80) was a lay member of the Dominican Order, a mystical author who was canonized in 1461. Chesterton here is referring to the time when Catherine comforted a Perugian knight in prison, went with him to the scaffold, and then received his severed head in her hands.

[33] George Cadbury (1839–1922) was the proprietor of the *Daily News*, to which Chesterton regularly contributed. He is best known today as the founder of Cadbury's cocoa and chocolate company.

[34] John D. Rockefeller (1839–1937) was an American business magnate and philanthropist, considered to be the wealthiest American of all time.

might be symbolized in the statement that white is a colour: not merely the absence of a colour. All that I am urging here can be expressed by saying that Christianity sought in most of these cases to keep two colours coexistent but pure. It is not a mixture like russet or purple; it is rather like a shot silk, for a shot silk is always at right angles, and is in the pattern of the cross.

So it is also, of course, with the contradictory charges of the anti-Christians about submission and slaughter. It *is* true that the Church told some men to fight and others not to fight; and it *is* true that those who fought were like thunderbolts and those who did not fight were like statues. All this simply means that the Church preferred to use its Supermen and to use its Tolstoyans. There must be *some* good in the life of battle, for so many good men have enjoyed being soldiers. There must be *some* good in the idea of non-resistance, for so many good men seem to enjoy being Quakers. All that the Church did (so far as that goes) was to prevent either of these good things from ousting the other. They existed side by side. The Tolstoyans, having all the scruples of monks, simply became monks. The Quakers became a club instead of becoming a sect. Monks said all that Tolstoy says; they poured out lucid lamentations about the cruelty of battles and the vanity of revenge. But the Tolstoyans are not quite right enough to run the whole world; and in the ages of faith they were not allowed to run it. The world did not lose the last charge of Sir James Douglas or the banner of Joan the Maid.[35]

And sometimes this pure gentleness and this pure fierceness met and justified their juncture; the paradox of all the prophets was fulfilled, and, in the soul of St. Louis,[36] the lion lay down with

---

[35] Sir James Douglas (1286–1330) was a Scottish knight and feudal lord who invaded England in 1319. He later set out on a pilgrimage to the Holy Land but was killed on the way. Joan the Maid is another name for Joan of Arc.

[36] Chesterton is likely referring to Louis IX (1214–70), king of France, who was known for his severity in punishing blasphemy and other social ills, as well as for his peacemaking efforts and introduction of the presumption of innocence in criminal procedure.

the lamb.[37] But remember that this text is too lightly interpreted. It is constantly assured, especially in our Tolstoyan tendencies, that when the lion lies down with the lamb the lion becomes lamb-like. But that is brutal annexation and imperialism on the part of the lamb. That is simply the lamb absorbing the lion instead of the lion eating the lamb. The real problem is—Can the lion lie down with the lamb and still retain his royal ferocity? *That* is the problem the Church attempted; *that* is the miracle she achieved.

Christianity and the Balancing of Apparent Accidents

This is what I have called guessing the hidden eccentricities of life. This is knowing that a man's heart is to the left and not in the middle. This is knowing not only that the earth is round, but knowing exactly where it is flat. Christian doctrine detected the oddities of life. It not only discovered the law, but it foresaw the exceptions.

Those underrate Christianity who say that it discovered mercy; any one might discover mercy. In fact every one did. But to discover a plan for being merciful and also severe—*that* was to anticipate a strange need of human nature. For no one wants to be forgiven for a big sin as if it were a little one. Any one might say that we should be neither quite miserable nor quite happy. But to find out how far one *may* be quite miserable without making it impossible to be quite happy—that was a discovery in psychology. Any one might say, "Neither swagger nor grovel"; and it would have been a limit. But to say, "Here you can swagger and there you can grovel"—that was an emancipation.

This was the big fact about Christian ethics; the discovery of the new balance. Paganism had been like a pillar of marble, upright because proportioned with symmetry. Christianity was like a huge and ragged and romantic rock, which, though it sways on

---

[37] Chesterton refers here to Isa 11:6–9, where the vision of the prophet shows the lion and the wolf dwelling in peace with the lamb, the leopard with the kid, and the calf with a young lion.

its pedestal at a touch, yet, because its exaggerated excrescences exactly balance each other, is enthroned there for a thousand years. In a Gothic cathedral the columns were all different, but they were all necessary. Every support seemed an accidental and fantastic support; every buttress was a flying buttress.

So in Christendom apparent accidents balanced. Becket wore a hair shirt under his gold and crimson, and there is much to be said for the combination; for Becket got the benefit of the hair shirt while the people in the street got the benefit of the crimson and gold. It is at least better than the manner of the modern millionaire, who has the black and the drab outwardly for others, and the gold next his heart. But the balance was not always in one man's body as in Becket's; the balance was often distributed over the whole body of Christendom. Because a man prayed and fasted on the Northern snows, flowers could be flung at his festival in the Southern cities; and because fanatics drank water on the sands of Syria, men could still drink cider in the orchards of England. This is what makes Christendom at once so much more perplexing and so much more interesting than the Pagan empire; just as Amiens Cathedral is not better but more interesting than the Parthenon.[38]

If any one wants a modern proof of all this, let him consider the curious fact that, under Christianity, Europe (while remaining a unity) has broken up into individual nations. Patriotism is a perfect example of this deliberate balancing of one emphasis against another emphasis. The instinct of the Pagan empire would have said, "You shall all be Roman citizens, and grow alike; let the German grow less slow and reverent; the Frenchmen less experimental and swift." But the instinct of Christian Europe says, "Let the German remain slow and reverent, that the Frenchman may the more safely be swift and experimental. We will make an equipoise out of these excesses.[39] The absurdity called Germany shall correct the insanity called France."

---

[38] Amiens Cathedral is a Gothic cathedral in Amiens, France. The Parthenon is a former temple in Greece.

[39] An equipoise is a balance of forces or interests.

The Thrilling Romance of Orthodoxy

Last and most important, it is exactly this which explains what is so inexplicable to all the modern critics of the history of Christianity. I mean the monstrous wars about small points of theology, the earthquakes of emotion about a gesture or a word. It was only a matter of an inch; but an inch is everything when you are balancing.

The Church could not afford to swerve a hair's breadth on some things if she was to continue her great and daring experiment of the irregular equilibrium. Once let one idea become less powerful and some other idea would become too powerful. It was no flock of sheep the Christian shepherd was leading, but a herd of bulls and tigers, of terrible ideals and devouring doctrines, each one of them strong enough to turn to a false religion and lay waste the world. Remember that the Church went in specifically for dangerous ideas; she was a lion tamer. The idea of birth through a Holy Spirit, of the death of a divine being, of the forgiveness of sins, or the fulfilment of prophecies, are ideas which, any one can see, need but a touch to turn them into something blasphemous or ferocious. The smallest link was let drop by the artificers of the Mediterranean, and the lion of ancestral pessimism burst his chain in the forgotten forests of the north.

Of these theological equalisations I have to speak afterwards. Here it is enough to notice that if some small mistake were made in doctrine, huge blunders might be made in human happiness. A sentence phrased wrong about the nature of symbolism would have broken all the best statues in Europe. A slip in the definitions might stop all the dances; might wither all the Christmas trees or break all the Easter eggs. Doctrines had to be defined within strict limits, even in order that man might enjoy general human liberties. The Church had to be careful, if only that the world might be careless.

This is the thrilling romance of Orthodoxy. People have fallen into a foolish habit of speaking of orthodoxy as something heavy, humdrum, and safe. There never was anything so perilous or so exciting as orthodoxy. It was sanity: and to be sane is more dramatic than to be mad. It was the equilibrium of a man behind madly rushing horses, seeming to stoop this way and to sway that, yet in every attitude having the grace of statuary and the accuracy of arithmetic. The Church in its early days went fierce and fast with any warhorse; yet it is utterly unhistoric to say that she merely went mad along one idea, like a vulgar fanaticism. She swerved to left and right, so exactly as to avoid enormous obstacles. She left on one hand the huge bulk of Arianism,[40] buttressed by all the worldly powers to make Christianity too worldly. The next instant she was swerving to avoid an orientalism, which would have made it too unworldly.

The orthodox Church never took the tame course or accepted the conventions; the orthodox Church was never respectable. It would have been easier to have accepted the earthly power of the Arians. It would have been easy, in the Calvinistic seventeenth century, to fall into the bottomless pit of predestination. It is easy to be a madman: it is easy to be a heretic. It is always easy to let the age have its head; the difficult thing is to keep one's own. It is always easy to be a modernist; as it is easy to be a snob.

To have fallen into any of those open traps of error and exaggeration which fashion after fashion and sect after sect set along the historic path of Christendom—that would indeed have been simple. It is always simple to fall; there are an infinity of angles at which one falls, only one at which one stands. To have fallen into any one of the fads from Gnosticism to Christian Science would indeed have been obvious and tame. But to have avoided them all has been one whirling adventure; and in my vision the heavenly chariot flies thundering through the ages, the dull heresies sprawling and prostrate, the wild truth reeling but erect.

---

[40] Arianism is the heresy that denies the divinity of Jesus Christ.

Chapter Summary

Chesterton opened this chapter by claiming there is a logic to the world and to humanity, but at the point you'd expect something to be the case (a human having two hearts, since the body appears to be divided evenly into two), we find a "silent swerving" from accuracy. It is the "uncanny element in everything," he wrote. Applying this insight to Christianity, Chesterton found the Christian creed also displayed this oddity—a strangeness that corresponds to the world.

What prompted Chesterton's journey from paganism to agnosticism to Christianity was not his reading of Christian apologetics but the doubts he discovered while reading the *critics* of Christianity. Time after time he watched how agnostics and freethinkers lashed out at the Christian creed for contradictory reasons (too gloomy, yet too rose-colored; too meek, yet too warlike; too exclusive, yet too inclusive; too simple, yet too pompous, etc.). Having surveyed all of these opposing criticisms, Chesterton came to the conclusion that perhaps Christianity was *right* and all the critics were *wrong*, and their criticisms reflected more of their own weaknesses than Christianity's. From there, Chesterton reviewed the basics of Christian orthodoxy and ethics, recognizing the power in these paradoxes—the holding together of fierce and apparently opposing passions and virtues. Why did Christianity embrace "parallel passions" and insist on precision in doctrine? In order to maintain its balance and to set free the world, for "if some small mistake were made in doctrine, huge blunders might be made in human happiness."

Discussion Questions

- What oddities and irregularities do you see in the world?
- What major criticisms are launched against Christianity today? How does Chesterton's approach to paradox address them?

- Can you think of other examples of paradox in Christian theology and ethics?
- Why does Chesterton believe the church is right to insist on small points of doctrine?

SEVEN

"The Eternal Revolution" marks the moment when Chesterton takes the Christian vision of history and the world and shows how it contrasts with idealistic visions of progress that always change the standard. Earlier in *Orthodoxy*, Chesterton claimed that lasting reform can only take place when we hate the world enough to believe it should be changed but also love the world enough to want to change it. Building on this idea, Chesterton says Christians are indeed fond of this world, enough to try to change it, but they are even more committed to another world, which provides the standard or ideal into which this world should be changed. Thus, Christianity turns out to be an ever-renewing series of revolutions and the basis for democracy in society.

Chesterton's goal in this chapter is to explore the notion of progress by showing us the necessity of having an ideal—a standard—that is fixed. This ideal provides the goal and the basis for all reform in society, and it also helps us see why Christians must be ever "watchful," since even the best attempts at changing the world can easily backfire and slide back into sin and selfishness. He then seeks to demonstrate why the pillars of democracy (over against aristocracy that benefits the rich and powerful) are upheld by Christian teaching on the fallen state of mankind. In the end, he will argue that we must seek an eternal revolution against the "progress" of the world, and work instead toward the ideal of the New Jerusalem.

Memorable Parts to Look For

- Progress as changing the world to suit the vision versus "progress" as changing the vision
- The illustration of keeping a post white by painting it again and again
- Christianity's foundation for critiquing the aristocracy of the rich
- Pride as the downward drag of all things into solemnity

The Eternal Revolution

The following propositions have been urged:

1. First, that some faith in our life is required even to improve it;
2. second, that some dissatisfaction with things as they are is necessary even in order to be satisfied;
3. third, that to have this necessary content and necessary discontent it is not sufficient to have the obvious equilibrium of the Stoic. For mere resignation has neither the gigantic levity of pleasure nor the superb intolerance of pain.

There is a vital objection to the advice merely to grin and bear it. The objection is that if you merely bear it, you do not grin. Greek heroes do not grin: but gargoyles do—because they are Christian. And when a Christian is pleased, he is (in the most exact sense) frightfully pleased; his pleasure is frightful. Christ prophesied the whole of Gothic architecture in that hour when nervous and respectable people (such people as now object to barrel organs) objected to the shouting of the gutter-snipes of Jerusalem. He said, "If these were silent, the very stones would cry out."[1] Under the impulse of His spirit arose like a clamorous chorus the facades of

[1] Luke 19:40.

the mediaeval cathedrals, thronged with shouting faces and open mouths. The prophecy has fulfilled itself: the very stones cry out.

The Importance of the Ideal

If these things be conceded, though only for argument, we may take up where we left it the thread of the thought of the natural man, called by the Scotch (with regrettable familiarity), "The Old Man." We can ask the next question so obviously in front of us. Some satisfaction is needed even to make things better. But what do we mean by making things better?

Most modern talk on this matter is a mere argument in a circle—that circle which we have already made the symbol of madness and of mere rationalism. Evolution is only good if it produces good; good is only good if it helps evolution. The elephant stands on the tortoise, and the tortoise on the elephant.

An Ideal Based on Nature?

Obviously, it will not do to take our ideal from the principle in nature; for the simple reason that (except for some human or divine theory), there is no principle in nature. For instance, the cheap anti-democrat of today will tell you solemnly that there is no equality in nature. He is right, but he does not see the logical addendum. There is no equality in nature; also there is no inequality in nature. Inequality, as much as equality, implies a standard of value.

To read aristocracy into the anarchy of animals is just as sentimental as to read democracy into it. Both aristocracy and democracy are human ideals: the one saying that all men are valuable, the other that some men are more valuable. But nature does not say that cats are more valuable than mice; nature makes no remark on the subject. She does not even say that the cat is enviable or the mouse pitiable. We think the cat superior because we have (or most of us have) a particular philosophy to the effect that life is better than death. But if the mouse were a German pessimist mouse, he might not think that the cat had beaten him at all. He might think he had beaten the cat by getting to the grave first. Or he might feel that he had actually inflicted frightful punishment on the cat by keeping him alive. Just as a microbe might feel proud of spreading a pestilence, so the pessimistic mouse might exult to think that he was renewing in the cat the torture of conscious existence. It all depends on the philosophy of the mouse. You cannot even say that there is victory or superiority in nature unless you have some doctrine about what things are superior. You cannot even say that the cat scores unless there is a system of scoring. You cannot even say that the cat gets the best of it unless there is some best to be got.

We cannot, then, get the ideal itself from nature, and as we follow here the first and natural speculation, we will leave out (for the present) the idea of getting it from God. We must have our own vision. But the attempts of most moderns to express it are highly vague.

An Ideal Based on the Passage of Time?

Some fall back simply on the clock: they talk as if mere passage through time brought some superiority; so that even a man of the first mental calibre carelessly uses the phrase that human morality is never up to date. How can anything be up to date?—a date has no character. How can one say that Christmas celebrations are not suitable to the twenty-fifth of a month? What the writer meant, of course, was that the majority is behind his favourite minority—or in front of it.

An Ideal Based on Metaphors?

Other vague modern people take refuge in material metaphors; in fact, this is the chief mark of vague modern people. Not daring to define their doctrine of what is good, they use physical figures of speech without stint or shame, and, what is worst of all, seem to think these cheap analogies are exquisitely spiritual and superior to the old morality. Thus they think it intellectual to talk about things being "high." It is at least the reverse of intellectual; it is a mere phrase from a steeple or a weathercock. "Tommy was a good boy" is a pure philosophical statement, worthy of Plato or Aquinas. "Tommy lived the higher life" is a gross metaphor from a ten-foot rule.

This, incidentally, is almost the whole weakness of Nietzsche, whom some are representing as a bold and strong thinker. No one will deny that he was a poetical and suggestive thinker; but he was quite the reverse of strong. He was not at all bold. He never put his own meaning before himself in bald abstract words: as did Aristotle and Calvin, and even Karl Marx, the hard, fearless men of thought. Nietzsche always escaped a question by a physical metaphor, like a cheery minor poet. He said, "beyond good and evil,"[2] because he had not the courage to say, "more good than good and evil," or, "more evil than good and evil." Had he faced his thought without metaphors, he would have seen that it was nonsense. So, when he describes his hero, he does not dare to say, "the purer man," or "the happier man," or "the sadder man," for all these are ideas; and ideas are alarming. He says "the upper man," or "over man," a physical metaphor from acrobats or alpine climbers. Nietzsche is truly a very timid thinker. He does not really know in the least what sort of man he wants evolution to produce. And if he does not know, certainly the ordinary evolutionists, who talk about things being "higher," do not know either.

Then again, some people fall back on sheer submission and sitting still. Nature is going to do something some day; nobody knows what, and nobody knows when. We have no reason for acting, and no reason for not acting. If anything happens it is right: if anything is prevented it was wrong.

---

[2] *Beyond Good and Evil* is the title of Nietzsche's book published in 1886.

Again, some people try to anticipate nature by doing something, by doing anything. Because we may possibly grow wings they cut off their legs. Yet nature may be trying to make them centipedes for all they know.

An Ideal Tied to a Definite Vision

Lastly, there is a fourth class of people who take whatever it is that they happen to want, and say that that is the ultimate aim of evolution. And these are the only sensible people. This is the only really healthy way with the word *evolution*, to work for what you want, and to call *that* evolution. The only intelligible sense that progress or advance can have among men, is that we have a definite vision, and that we wish to make the whole world like that vision.

If you like to put it so, the essence of the doctrine is that what we have around us is the mere method and preparation for something that we have to create. This is not a world, but rather the material for a world. God has given us not so much the colours of a picture as the colours of a palette. But he has also given us a subject, a model, a fixed vision. We must be clear about what we want to paint.

The Ideal as Necessary for Reform

This adds a further principle to our previous list of principles. We have said we must be fond of this world, even in order to change it. We now add that we must be fond of another world (real or imaginary) in order to have something to change it to.

We need not debate about the mere words *evolution* or *progress*: personally I prefer to call it reform. For reform implies form. It implies that we are trying to shape the world in a particular image; to make it something that we see already in our minds. Evolution is a metaphor from mere automatic unrolling. Progress is a metaphor from merely walking along a road—very likely the wrong road. But reform is a metaphor for reasonable and determined men: it means that we see a certain thing out of shape and we mean to put it into shape. And we know what shape.

Two Conceptions of Progress

Now here comes in the whole collapse and huge blunder of our age. We have mixed up two different things, two opposite things. Progress should mean that we are always changing the world to suit the vision. Progress does mean (just now) that we are always changing the vision.

It should mean that we are slow but sure in bringing justice and mercy among men: it does mean that we are very swift in doubting the desirability of justice and mercy: a wild page from any Prussian sophist makes men doubt it.[3]

Progress should mean that we are always walking towards the New Jerusalem. It does mean that the New Jerusalem is always walking away from us. We are not altering the real to suit the ideal. We are altering the ideal: it is easier.

Silly examples are always simpler; let us suppose a man wanted a particular kind of world; say, a blue world. He would have no cause to complain of the slightness or swiftness of his task; he might toil for a long time at the transformation; he could work away (in every sense) until all was blue. He could have heroic adventures; the putting of the last touches to a blue tiger. He could have fairy dreams; the dawn of a blue moon. But if he worked hard, that high-minded reformer would certainly (from his own point of view) leave the world better and bluer than he found it. If he altered a blade of grass to his favourite colour every day, he would get on slowly. But if he altered his favourite colour every day, he would not get on at all. If, after reading a fresh philosopher, he started to paint everything

[3] A sophist was a specific kind of teacher in ancient Greece, now often used to refer to someone who reasons with clever but fallacious arguments.

red or yellow, his work would be thrown away: there would be nothing to show except a few blue tigers walking about, specimens of his early bad manner.

This is exactly the position of the average modern thinker. It will be said that this is avowedly a preposterous example. But it is literally the fact of recent history. The great and grave changes in our political civilization all belonged to the early nineteenth century, not to the later. They belonged to the black and white epoch when men believed fixedly in Toryism, in Protestantism, in Calvinism, in Reform, and not unfrequently in Revolution. And whatever each man believed in he hammered at steadily, without scepticism: and there was a time when the Established Church might have fallen, and the House of Lords nearly fell. It was because Radicals were wise enough to be constant and consistent; it was because Radicals were wise enough to be Conservative. But in the existing atmosphere there is not enough time and tradition in Radicalism to pull anything down.

There is a great deal of truth in Lord Hugh Cecil's suggestion (made in a fine speech) that the era of change is over, and that ours is an era of conservation and repose.[4] But probably it would pain Lord Hugh Cecil if he realized (what is certainly the case) that ours is only an age of conservation because it is an age of complete unbelief. Let beliefs fade fast and frequently, if you wish institutions to remain the same. The more the life of the mind is unhinged, the more the machinery of matter will be left to itself. The net result of all our political suggestions, Collectivism, Tolstoyanism, Neo-Feudalism, Communism, Anarchy, Scientific Bureaucracy—the plain fruit of all of them is that the Monarchy and the House of Lords will remain. The net result of all the new religions will be that the Church of England will not (for heaven knows how long) be disestablished. It was Karl Marx, Nietzsche, Tolstoy,

---

[4] Lord Hugh Cecil (1869–1956) was a politician in the British Conservative Party.

Cunninghame Grahame,[5] Bernard Shaw and Auberon Herbert,[6] who between them, with bowed gigantic backs, bore up the throne of the Archbishop of Canterbury.

We may say broadly that free thought is the best of all the safeguards against freedom. Managed in a modern style the emancipation of the slave's mind is the best way of preventing the emancipation of the slave. Teach him to worry about whether he wants to be free, and he will not free himself. Again, it may be said that this instance is remote or extreme. But, again, it is exactly true of the men in the streets around us. It is true that the negro slave, being a debased barbarian, will probably have either a human affection of loyalty, or a human affection for liberty. But the man we see every day—the worker in Mr. Gradgrind's factory, the little clerk in Mr. Gradgrind's office—he is too mentally worried to believe in freedom.[7] He is kept quiet with revolutionary literature. He is calmed and kept in his place by a constant succession of wild philosophies. He is a Marxian one day, a Nietzscheite the next day, a Superman (probably) the next day; and a slave every day. The only thing that remains after all the philosophies is the factory. The only man who gains by all the philosophies is Gradgrind. It would be worth his while to keep his commercial helotry supplied with sceptical literature.[8] And now I come to think of it, of course, Gradgrind is famous for giving libraries. He shows his sense. All modern books are on his side.

---

[5] Robert Bontine Cunninghame Graham (1852–1936) was a Scottish politician, writer, journalist, and adventurer. He was a socialist.

[6] Auberon Herbert (1838–1906) was a political philosopher and author. A secularist and agnostic, he promoted a classical liberal philosophy.

[7] Mr. Thomas Gradgrind is a character in Charles Dickens's novel *Hard Times* (1854). He is the school board superintendent obsessed with facts and whatever is practical. His name now is used generically to refer to someone who is hard and only concerned with cold facts and numbers.

[8] *Helotry* is another word for serfdom or slavery.

The Ideal Must Be Fixed

As long as the vision of heaven is always changing, the vision of earth will be exactly the same. No ideal will remain long enough to be realized, or even partly realized. The modern young man will never change his environment; for he will always change his mind.

This, therefore, is our first requirement about the ideal towards which progress is directed; it must be fixed. Whistler used to make many rapid studies of a sitter;[9] it did not matter if he tore up twenty portraits. But it would matter if he looked up twenty times, and each time saw a new person sitting placidly for his portrait. So it does not matter (comparatively speaking) how often humanity fails to imitate its ideal; for then all its old failures are fruitful. But it does frightfully matter how often humanity changes its ideal; for then all its old failures are fruitless.

The Fixed Ideal and Revolution

The question therefore becomes this: How can we keep the artist discontented with his pictures while preventing him from being vitally discontented with his art? How can we make a man always dissatisfied with his work, yet always satisfied with working? How can we make sure that the portrait painter will throw the portrait out of window instead of taking the natural and more human course of throwing the sitter out of window?

A strict rule is not only necessary for ruling; it is also necessary for rebelling. This fixed and familiar ideal is necessary to any sort of revolution. Man will sometimes act slowly upon new ideas; but he will only act swiftly upon old ideas. If I am merely to float or fade or evolve, it may be towards something anarchic; but if I am to riot, it must be for something respectable.

---

[9] James Whistler (1834–1903) was an American artist during the Gilded Age and a leading proponent of "art for art's sake."

The Need for an Eternal Test

This is the whole weakness of certain schools of progress and moral evolution. They suggest that there has been a slow movement towards morality, with an imperceptible ethical change in every year or at every instant. There is only one great disadvantage in this theory. It talks of a slow movement towards justice; but it does not permit a swift movement. A man is not allowed to leap up and declare a certain state of things to be intrinsically intolerable.

To make the matter clear, it is better to take a specific example. Certain of the idealistic vegetarians, such as Mr. Salt,[10] say that the time has now come for eating no meat; by implication they assume that at one time it was right to eat meat, and they suggest (in words that could be quoted) that some day it may be wrong to eat milk and eggs. I do not discuss here the question of what is justice to animals. I only say that whatever is justice ought, under given conditions, to be prompt justice. If an animal is wronged, we ought to be able to rush to his rescue.

But how can we rush if we are, perhaps, in advance of our time? How can we rush to catch a train which may not arrive for a few centuries? How can I denounce a man for skinning cats, if he is only now what I may possibly become in drinking a glass of milk? A splendid and insane Russian sect ran about taking all the cattle out of all the carts. How can I pluck up courage to take the horse out of my hansom-cab, when I do not know whether my evolutionary watch is only a little fast or the cabman's a little slow?

Suppose I say to a sweater, "Slavery suited one stage of evolution."

And suppose he answers, "And sweating suits this stage of evolution."

How can I answer if there is no eternal test? If sweaters can be behind the current morality, why should not philanthropists be

---

[10] Henry Salt (1851–1939) was an English writer and campaigner for social reform, including animal rights. His book *A Plea for Vegetarianism* was published in 1886.

in front of it? What on earth is the current morality, except in its literal sense—the morality that is always running away?

Thus we may say that a permanent ideal is as necessary to the innovator as to the conservative; it is necessary whether we wish the king's orders to be promptly executed or whether we only wish the king to be promptly executed. The guillotine has many sins, but to do it justice there is nothing evolutionary about it. The favourite evolutionary argument finds its best answer in the axe. The Evolutionist says, "Where do you draw the line?" the Revolutionist answers, "I draw it *here*: exactly between your head and body." There must at any given moment be an abstract right and wrong if any blow is to be struck; there must be something eternal if there is to be anything sudden. Therefore for all intelligible human purposes, for altering things or for keeping things as they are, for founding a system forever, as in China, or for altering it every month as in the early French Revolution, it is equally necessary that the vision should be a fixed vision. This is our first requirement.

Christianity as an Eternal Ideal

When I had written this down, I felt once again the presence of something else in the discussion: as a man hears a church bell above the sound of the street.

Something seemed to be saying, "My ideal at least is fixed; for it was fixed before the foundations of the world. My vision of perfection assuredly cannot be altered; for it is called Eden. You may alter the place to which you are going; but you cannot alter the place from which you have come. To the orthodox there must always be a case for revolution; for in the hearts of men God has been put under the feet of Satan. In the upper world hell once rebelled against heaven. But in this world heaven is rebelling against hell. For the orthodox there can always be a revolution; for a revolution is a restoration. At any instant you may strike a blow for the perfection which no man has seen since Adam. No unchanging custom, no changing evolution can make the original good any thing but good. Man may have had concubines as long as cows have had horns: still they are not a part of him if they are sinful. Men may have been under oppression ever since fish were under water; still they ought not to be, if oppression is sinful. The chain may seem as natural to the slave, or the paint to the harlot, as does the plume to the bird or the burrow to the fox; still they are not, if they are sinful. I lift my prehistoric legend to defy all your history. Your vision is not merely a fixture: it is a fact." I paused to note the new coincidence of Christianity: but I passed on.

The Nature of Progress and Evidence of Design

I passed on to the next necessity of any ideal of progress. Some people (as we have said) seem to believe in an automatic and impersonal progress in the nature of things. But it is clear that no political activity can be encouraged by saying that progress is natural and inevitable; that is not a reason for being active, but rather a reason for being lazy. If we are bound to improve, we need not trouble to improve. The pure doctrine of progress is the best of all reasons for not being a progressive. But it is to none of these obvious comments that I wish primarily to call attention.

The only arresting point is this: that if we suppose improvement to be natural, it must be fairly simple. The world might conceivably be working towards one consummation, but hardly towards any particular arrangement of many qualities.

To take our original simile: Nature by herself may be growing more blue; that is, a process so simple that it might be impersonal. But Nature cannot be making a careful picture made of many picked colours, unless Nature is personal. If the end of the world were mere darkness or mere light it might come as slowly and inevitably as dusk or dawn. But if the end of the world is to be a piece of elaborate and artistic chiaroscuro, then there must be design in it, either human or divine. The world, through mere time, might grow black like an old picture, or white like an old coat; but if it is turned into a particular piece of black and white art—then there is an artist.

Humanitarian Progress?

If the distinction be not evident, I give an ordinary instance. We constantly hear a particularly cosmic creed from the modern humanitarians; I use the word *humanitarian* in the ordinary sense, as meaning one who upholds the claims of all creatures against those of humanity. They suggest that through the ages we have been growing more and more humane, that is to say, that one after another, groups or sections of beings, slaves, children, women, cows, or what not, have been gradually admitted to mercy or to justice. They say that we once thought it right to eat men (we didn't); but I am not here concerned with their history, which is highly unhistorical. As a fact, anthropophagy is certainly a decadent thing,[11] not a primitive one. It is much more likely that modern men will eat human flesh out of affectation than that primitive man ever ate it out of ignorance.

I am here only following the outlines of their argument, which consists in maintaining that man has been progressively more lenient, first to citizens, then to slaves, then to animals, and then (presumably) to plants. I think it wrong to sit on a man. Soon, I shall think it wrong to sit on a horse. Eventually (I suppose) I shall think it wrong to sit on a chair. That is the drive of the argument. And for this argument it can be said that it is possible to talk of it in terms of evolution or inevitable progress. A perpetual tendency to touch fewer and fewer things might—one feels, be a mere brute unconscious tendency, like that of a species to produce fewer and fewer children. This drift may be really evolutionary, because it is stupid.

---

[11] Anthropophagy is the eating of human flesh by human beings.

One's View of Nature

Darwinism can be used to back up two mad moralities, but it cannot be used to back up a single sane one. The kinship and competition of all living creatures can be used as a reason for being insanely cruel or insanely sentimental; but not for a healthy love of animals. On the evolutionary basis you may be inhumane, or you may be absurdly humane; but you cannot be human. That you and a tiger are one may be a reason for being tender to a tiger. Or it may be a reason for being as cruel as the tiger. It is one way to train the tiger to imitate you, it is a shorter way to imitate the tiger. But in neither case does evolution tell you how to treat a tiger reasonably, that is, to admire his stripes while avoiding his claws.

If you want to treat a tiger reasonably, you must go back to the garden of Eden. For the obstinate reminder continued to recur: only the supernatural has taken a sane view of Nature. The essence of all pantheism, evolutionism, and modern cosmic religion is really in this proposition: that Nature is our mother. Unfortunately, if you regard Nature as a mother, you discover that she is a stepmother.

The main point of Christianity was this: that Nature is not our mother: Nature is our sister. We can be proud of her beauty, since we have the same father; but she has no authority over us; we have to admire, but not to imitate. This gives to the typically Christian pleasure in this earth a strange touch of lightness that is almost frivolity. Nature was a solemn mother to the worshippers of Isis and Cybele.[12] Nature was a solemn mother to Wordsworth or to Emerson. But Nature is not solemn to Francis of Assisi or to George Herbert. To St. Francis, Nature is a sister, and even a younger sister: a little, dancing sister, to be laughed at as well as loved.

---

[12] Isis was one of the most important goddesses of ancient Egypt. Cybele was the ancient Phrygian Mother of the Gods, a primal nature goddess.

Proportion as Evidence for Design

This, however, is hardly our main point at present; I have admitted it only in order to show how constantly, and as it were accidentally, the key would fit the smallest doors. Our main point is here, that if there be a mere trend of impersonal improvement in Nature, it must presumably be a simple trend towards some simple triumph. One can imagine that some automatic tendency in biology might work for giving us longer and longer noses. But the question is, do we want to have longer and longer noses? I fancy not; I believe that we most of us want to say to our noses, "thus far, and no farther; and here shall thy proud point be stayed:" we require a nose of such length as may ensure an interesting face. But we cannot imagine a mere biological trend towards producing interesting faces; because an interesting face is one particular arrangement of eyes, nose, and mouth, in a most complex relation to each other.

Proportion cannot be a drift: it is either an accident or a design. So with the ideal of human morality and its relation to the humanitarians and the anti-humanitarians. It is conceivable that we are going more and more to keep our hands off things: not to drive horses; not to pick flowers. We may eventually be bound not to disturb a man's mind even by argument; not to disturb the sleep of birds even by coughing. The ultimate apotheosis would appear to be that of a man sitting quite still, nor daring to stir for fear of disturbing a fly, nor to eat for fear of incommoding a microbe. To so crude a consummation as that we might perhaps unconsciously drift. But do we want so crude a consummation? Similarly, we might unconsciously evolve along the opposite or Nietzschian line of development—superman crushing superman in one tower of tyrants until the universe is smashed up for fun. But do we want the universe smashed up for fun?

Is it not quite clear that what we really hope for is one particular management and proposition of these two things; a certain amount of restraint and respect, a certain amount of energy and mastery? If our life is ever really as beautiful as a fairy-tale, we shall have to remember that all the beauty of a fairy-tale lies in this: that the prince has a wonder which just stops short of being fear. If he is afraid of the giant, there is an end of him; but also if he is not astonished at the giant, there is an end of the fairy-tale. The whole point depends upon his being at once humble enough to wonder, and haughty enough to defy.

So our attitude to the giant of the world must not merely be increasing delicacy or increasing contempt: it must be one particular proportion of the two—which is exactly right. We must have in us enough reverence for all things outside us to make us tread fearfully on the grass. We must also have enough disdain for all things outside us, to make us, on due occasion, spit at the stars.

Yet these two things (if we are to be good or happy) must be combined, not in any combination, but in one particular combination. The perfect happiness of men on the earth (if it ever comes) will not be a flat and solid thing, like the satisfaction of animals. It will be an exact and perilous balance; like that of a desperate romance. Man must have just enough faith in himself to have adventures, and just enough doubt of himself to enjoy them.

The Personal Artist

This, then, is our second requirement for the ideal of progress. First, it must be fixed; second, it must be composite. It must not (if it is to satisfy our souls) be the mere victory of some one thing swallowing up everything else, love or pride or peace or adventure; it must be a definite picture composed of these elements in their best proportion and relation.

I am not concerned at this moment to deny that some such good culmination may be, by the constitution of things, reserved for the human race. I only point out that if this composite happiness is fixed for us it must be fixed by some mind; for only a mind can place the exact proportions of a composite happiness. If the beatification of the world is a mere work of nature, then it must be as simple as the freezing of the world, or the burning up of the world. But if the beatification of the world is not a work of nature but a work of art, then it involves an artist.

And here again my contemplation was cloven by the ancient voice which said, "I could have told you all this a long time ago. If there is any certain progress it can only be my kind of progress, the progress towards a complete city of virtues and dominations where righteousness and peace contrive to kiss each other. An impersonal force might be leading you to a wilderness of perfect flatness or a peak of perfect height. But only a personal God can possibly be leading you (if, indeed, you are being led) to a city with just streets and architectural proportions, a city in which each of you can contribute exactly the right amount of your own colour to the many coloured coat of Joseph."

Twice again, therefore, Christianity had come in with the exact answer that I required. I had said, "The ideal must be fixed," and the Church had answered, "Mine is literally fixed, for it existed before anything else."

I said secondly, "It must be artistically combined, like a picture"; and the Church answered, "Mine is quite literally a picture, for I know who painted it."

Then I went on to the third thing, which, as it seemed to me, was needed for an Utopia or goal of progress. And of all the three it is infinitely the hardest to express. Perhaps it might be put thus: that we need watchfulness even in Utopia, lest we fall from Utopia as we fell from Eden.

The Vigilance Required for the Eternal Revolution

We have remarked that one reason offered for being a progressive is that things naturally tend to grow better. But the only real reason for being a progressive is that things naturally tend to grow worse. The corruption in things is not only the best argument for being progressive; it is also the only argument against being conservative.

The conservative theory would really be quite sweeping and unanswerable if it were not for this one fact. But all conservatism is based upon the idea that if you leave things alone you leave them as they are. But you do not. If you leave a thing alone you leave it to a torrent of change. If you leave a white post alone it will soon be a black post. If you particularly want it to be white you must be always painting it again; that is, you must be always having a revolution. Briefly, if you want the old white post you must have a new white post.

But this which is true even of inanimate things is in a quite special and terrible sense true of all human things. An almost unnatural vigilance is really required of the citizen because of the horrible rapidity with which human institutions grow old. It is the custom in passing romance and journalism to talk of men suffering under old tyrannies. But, as a fact, men have almost always suffered under new tyrannies; under tyrannies that had been public liberties hardly twenty years before. Thus England went mad with joy over the patriotic monarchy of Elizabeth;[13] and then (almost immediately afterwards) went mad with rage in the trap of the tyranny of Charles the First.[14] So, again, in France the monarchy became intolerable, not just after it had been tolerated, but just after it had been adored. The son of Louis the well-beloved was Louis the guillotined.[15] So in the same way in England in the nineteenth century the Radical manufacturer was entirely trusted as a mere tribune of the people, until suddenly we heard the cry of the Socialist that he was a tyrant eating the people like bread. So again, we have almost up to the last instant trusted the newspapers as organs of public opinion. Just recently some of us have seen (not slowly, but with a start) that they are obviously nothing of the kind. They are, by the nature of the case, the hobbies of a few rich men.

---

[13] Queen Elizabeth I (1533–1603) reigned from 1558 to 1603.

[14] King Charles I (1600–1649) was king of England from 1625 until his execution in 1649.

[15] King Louis XV (1710–74) reigned over France for nearly fifty-nine years and was known as "Louis the Beloved." His son, King Louis XVI (1754–93), was executed by means of the guillotine, a major event of the French Revolution in 1793.

We have not any need to rebel against antiquity; we have to rebel against novelty. It is the new rulers, the capitalist or the editor, who really hold up the modern world. There is no fear that a modern king will attempt to override the constitution; it is more likely that he will ignore the constitution and work behind its back; he will take no advantage of his kingly power; it is more likely that he will take advantage of his kingly powerlessness, of the fact that he is free from criticism and publicity. For the king is the most private person of our time. It will not be necessary for any one to fight again against the proposal of a censorship of the press. We do not need a censorship of the press. We have a censorship by the press.

Christianity and the Fall

This startling swiftness with which popular systems turn oppressive is the third fact for which we shall ask our perfect theory of progress to allow. It must always be on the look out for every privilege being abused, for every working right becoming a wrong. In this matter I am entirely on the side of the revolutionists. They are really right to be always suspecting human institutions; they are right not to put their trust in princes nor in any child of man. The chieftain chosen to be the friend of the people becomes the enemy of the people; the newspaper started to tell the truth now exists to prevent the truth being told. Here, I say, I felt that I was really at last on the side of the revolutionary. And then I caught my breath again: for I remembered that I was once again on the side of the orthodox.

Christianity spoke again and said: "I have always maintained that men were naturally backsliders; that human virtue tended of its own nature to rust or to rot; I have always said that human beings as such go wrong, especially happy human beings, especially proud and prosperous human beings. This eternal revolution, this suspicion sustained through centuries, you (being a vague modern) call the doctrine of progress. If you were a philosopher you would call it, as I do, the doctrine of original sin. You may call it the cosmic advance as much as you like; I call it what it is—the Fall."

Christianity versus the Aristocracy

I have spoken of orthodoxy coming in like a sword; here I confess it came in like a battle-axe. For really (when I came to think of it) Christianity is the only thing left that has any real right to question the power of the well-nurtured or the well-bred.

I have listened often enough to Socialists, or even to democrats, saying that the physical conditions of the poor must of necessity make them mentally and morally degraded. I have listened to scientific men (and there are still scientific men not opposed to democracy) saying that if we give the poor healthier conditions vice and wrong will disappear. I have listened to them with a horrible attention, with a hideous fascination. For it was like watching a man energetically sawing from the tree the branch he is sitting on. If these happy democrats could prove their case, they would strike democracy dead. If the poor are thus utterly demoralized, it may or may not be practical to raise them. But it is certainly quite practical to disfranchise them.

If the man with a bad bedroom cannot give a good vote, then the first and swiftest deduction is that he shall give no vote. The governing class may not unreasonably say: "It may take us some time to reform his bedroom. But if he is the brute you say, it will take him very little time to ruin our country. Therefore we will take your hint and not give him the chance."

It fills me with horrible amusement to observe the way in which the earnest Socialist industriously lays the foundation of all aristocracy, expatiating blandly upon the evident unfitness of the poor to rule. It is like listening to somebody at an evening party apologising for entering without evening dress, and explaining that he had recently been intoxicated, had a personal habit of taking off his clothes in the street, and had, moreover, only just changed from prison uniform. At any moment, one feels, the host might say that really, if it was as bad as that, he need not come in at all. So it is when the ordinary Socialist, with a beaming face, proves that the poor, after their smashing experiences, cannot be really trustworthy. At any moment the rich may say, "Very well, then, we won't trust them," and bang the door in his face.

On the basis of Mr. Blatchford's view of heredity and environment, the case for the aristocracy is quite overwhelming. If clean homes and clean air make clean souls, why not give the power (for the present at any rate) to those who undoubtedly have the clean air? If better conditions will make the poor more fit to govern themselves, why should not better conditions already make the rich more fit to govern them? On the ordinary environment argument the matter is fairly manifest. The comfortable class must be merely our vanguard in Utopia.

Is there any answer to the proposition that those who have had the best opportunities will probably be our best guides? Is there any answer to the argument that those who have breathed clean air had better decide for those who have breathed foul? As far as I know, there is only one answer, and that answer is Christianity. Only the Christian Church can offer any rational objection to a complete confidence in the rich. For she has maintained from the beginning that the danger was not in man's environment, but in man.

Further, she has maintained that if we come to talk of a dangerous environment, the most dangerous environment of all is the commodious environment. I know that the most modern manufacture has been really occupied in trying to produce an abnormally large needle. I know that the most recent biologists have been chiefly anxious to discover a very small camel. But if we diminish the camel to his smallest, or open the eye of the needle to its largest—if, in short, we assume the words of Christ to have meant the very least that they could mean, His words must at the very least mean this—that rich men are not very likely to be morally trustworthy.[16]

Christianity even when watered down is hot enough to boil all modern society to rags. The mere minimum of the Church would be a deadly ultimatum to the world. For the whole modern world is

---

[16] Matt 19:24.

absolutely based on the assumption, not that the rich are necessary (which is tenable), but that the rich are trustworthy, which (for a Christian) is not tenable. You will hear everlastingly, in all discussions about newspapers, companies, aristocracies, or party politics, this argument that the rich man cannot be bribed. The fact is, of course, that the rich man is bribed; he has been bribed already. That is why he is a rich man.

The whole case for Christianity is that a man who is dependent upon the luxuries of this life is a corrupt man, spiritually corrupt, politically corrupt, financially corrupt. There is one thing that Christ and all the Christian saints have said with a sort of savage monotony. They have said simply that to be rich is to be in peculiar danger of moral wreck. It is not demonstrably un-Christian to kill the rich as violators of definable justice. It is not demonstrably un-Christian to crown the rich as convenient rulers of society. It is not certainly un-Christian to rebel against the rich or to submit to the rich. But it is quite certainly un-Christian to trust the rich, to regard the rich as more morally safe than the poor.

A Christian may consistently say, "I respect that man's rank, although he takes bribes." But a Christian cannot say, as all modern men are saying at lunch and breakfast, "a man of that rank would not take bribes." For it is a part of Christian dogma that any man in any rank may take bribes. It is a part of Christian dogma; it also happens by a curious coincidence that it is a part of obvious human history.

When people say that a man "in that position" would be incorruptible, there is no need to bring Christianity into the discussion. Was Lord Bacon a bootblack? Was the Duke of Marlborough a crossing sweeper?[17] In the best Utopia, I must be prepared for the moral fall of any man in any position at any moment; especially for my fall from my position at this moment.

---

[17] Francis Bacon (1561–1626) was tried for bribery and was fined and imprisoned. The first Duke of Marlborough (1650–1722) was accused of malversation and dismissed from his offices.

Christianity and Democracy

Much vague and sentimental journalism has been poured out to the effect that Christianity is akin to democracy, and most of it is scarcely strong or clear enough to refute the fact that the two things have often quarrelled. The real ground upon which Christianity and democracy are one is very much deeper. The one specially and peculiarly un-Christian idea is the idea of Carlyle—the idea that the man should rule who feels that he can rule. Whatever else is Christian, this is heathen. If our faith comments on government at all, its comment must be this—that the man should rule who does *not* think that he can rule. Carlyle's hero may say, "I will be king"; but the Christian saint must say *Nolo episcopari.*[18] If the great paradox of Christianity means anything, it means this—that we must take the crown in our hands, and go hunting in dry places and dark corners of the earth until we find the one man who feels himself unfit to wear it. Carlyle was quite wrong; we have not got to crown the exceptional man who knows he can rule. Rather we must crown the much more exceptional man who knows he can't.

Now, this is one of the two or three vital defences of working democracy. The mere machinery of voting is not democracy, though at present it is not easy to effect any simpler democratic method. But even the machinery of voting is profoundly Christian in this practical sense—that it is an attempt to get at the opinion of those who would be too modest to offer it. It is a mystical adventure; it is specially trusting those who do not trust themselves. That enigma is strictly peculiar to Christendom. There is nothing really humble about the abnegation of the Buddhist; the mild Hindu is mild, but he is not meek. But there is something psychologically Christian about the idea of seeking for the opinion of the obscure rather than taking the obvious course of accepting the opinion of the prominent.

[18] Latin for "I do not wish to be a bishop."

To say that voting is particularly Christian may seem somewhat curious. To say that canvassing is Christian may seem quite crazy. But canvassing is very Christian in its primary idea. It is encouraging the humble; it is saying to the modest man, "Friend, go up higher."[19] Or if there is some slight defect in canvassing, that is in its perfect and rounded piety, it is only because it may possibly neglect to encourage the modesty of the canvasser.

The Downward Drag of Pride

Aristocracy is not an institution: aristocracy is a sin; generally a very venial one. It is merely the drift or slide of men into a sort of natural pomposity and praise of the powerful, which is the most easy and obvious affair in the world. It is one of the hundred answers to the fugitive perversion of modern "force" that the promptest and boldest agencies are also the most fragile or full of sensibility. The swiftest things are the softest things. A bird is active, because a bird is soft. A stone is helpless, because a stone is hard. The stone must by its own nature go downwards, because hardness is weakness. The bird can of its nature go upwards, because fragility is force. In perfect force there is a kind of frivolity, an airiness that can maintain itself in the air.

Modern investigators of miraculous history have solemnly admitted that a characteristic of the great saints is their power of "levitation." They might go further; a characteristic of the great saints is their power of levity. Angels can fly because they can take themselves lightly.

This has been always the instinct of Christendom, and especially the instinct of Christian art. Remember how Fra Angelico represented all his angels, not only as birds, but almost as butterflies.[20]

---

[19] Luke 14:10, Jesus's instruction to take the lowest seat at a dinner gathering and to be urged to move higher.

[20] Fra Angelico (c. 1395–1455) was an Italian painter of the Early Renaissance.

Remember how the most earnest mediaeval art was full of light and fluttering draperies, of quick and capering feet. It was the one thing that the modern Pre-raphaelites could not imitate in the real Pre-raphaelites.[21] Burne-Jones could never recover the deep levity of the Middle Ages.[22] In the old Christian pictures the sky over every figure is like a blue or gold parachute. Every figure seems ready to fly up and float about in the heavens. The tattered cloak of the beggar will bear him up like the rayed plumes of the angels. But the kings in their heavy gold and the proud in their robes of purple will all of their nature sink downwards, for pride cannot rise to levity or levitation.

Pride is the downward drag of all things into an easy solemnity. One "settles down" into a sort of selfish seriousness; but one has to rise to a gay self-forgetfulness. A man "falls" into a brown study; he reaches up at a blue sky. Seriousness is not a virtue. It would be a heresy, but a much more sensible heresy, to say that seriousness is a vice. It is really a natural trend or lapse into taking one's self gravely, because it is the easiest thing to do. It is much easier to write a good *Times* leading article than a good joke in *Punch*.[23] For solemnity flows out of men naturally; but laughter is a leap. It is easy to be heavy: hard to be light. Satan fell by the force of gravity.

Now, it is the peculiar honour of Europe since it has been Christian that while it has had aristocracy it has always at the back of its heart treated aristocracy as a weakness—generally as a weakness that must be allowed for. If any one wishes to appreciate this point, let him go outside Christianity into some other philosophical atmosphere. Let him, for instance, compare the classes of Europe with

---

[21] The Pre-Raphaelite Brotherhood was a secret society of young artists formed in 1850 who wanted to return to the art forms and sincerity that they claimed existed before the time of Raphael (1483–1520).

[22] Edward Burne-Jones (1833–98) was a British artist and designer known for his design of stained-glass windows. He was associated with the Pre-Raphaelite movement.

[23] *Punch* was a British weekly magazine of humor and satire from 1841 to 1992.

the castes of India. There aristocracy is far more awful, because it is far more intellectual. It is seriously felt that the scale of classes is a scale of spiritual values; that the baker is better than the butcher in an invisible and sacred sense. But no Christianity, not even the most ignorant or perverse, ever suggested that a baronet was better than a butcher in that sacred sense. No Christianity, however ignorant or extravagant, ever suggested that a duke would not be damned.

In pagan society there may have been (I do not know) some such serious division between the free man and the slave. But in Christian society we have always thought the gentleman a sort of joke, though I admit that in some great crusades and councils he earned the right to be called a practical joke. But we in Europe never really and at the root of our souls took aristocracy seriously. It is only an occasional non-European alien (such as Dr. Oscar Levy,[24] the only intelligent Nietzscheite) who can even manage for a moment to take aristocracy seriously. It may be a mere patriotic bias, though I do not think so, but it seems to me that the English aristocracy is not only the type, but is the crown and flower of all actual aristocracies; it has all the oligarchical virtues as well as all the defects. It is casual, it is kind, it is courageous in obvious matters; but it has one great merit that overlaps even these. The great and very obvious merit of the English aristocracy is that nobody could possibly take it seriously.

Love and the Desire to Be Bound

In short, I had spelled out slowly, as usual, the need for an equal law in Utopia; and, as usual, I found that Christianity had been there before me. The whole history of my Utopia has the same amusing sadness. I was always rushing out of my architectural study with plans for a new turret only to find it sitting up there in the sunlight, shining, and a thousand years old. For me, in the ancient

[24] Oscar Levy (1867–1946) translated and edited a complete edition of Nietzsche's works in eighteen volumes between 1909 and 1912.

and partly in the modern sense, God answered the prayer, "Prevent us, O Lord, in all our doings."[25] Without vanity, I really think there was a moment when I could have invented the marriage vow (as an institution) out of my own head; but I discovered, with a sigh, that it had been invented already. But, since it would be too long a business to show how, fact by fact and inch by inch, my own conception of Utopia was only answered in the New Jerusalem, I will take this one case of the matter of marriage as indicating the converging drift, I may say the converging crash of all the rest.

When the ordinary opponents of Socialism talk about impossibilities and alterations in human nature, they always miss an important distinction. In modern ideal conceptions of society there are some desires that are possibly not attainable: but there are some desires that are not desirable. That all men should live in equally beautiful houses is a dream that may or may not be attained. But that all men should live in the same beautiful house is not a dream at all; it is a nightmare. That a man should love all old women is an ideal that may not be attainable. But that a man should regard all old women exactly as he regards his mother is not only an unattainable ideal, but an ideal which ought not to be attained.

I do not know if the reader agrees with me in these examples; but I will add the example which has always affected me most. I could never conceive or tolerate any Utopia which did not leave to me the liberty for which I chiefly care, the liberty to bind myself. Complete anarchy would not merely make it impossible to have any discipline or fidelity; it would also make it impossible to have any fun. To take an obvious instance, it would not be worth while to bet if a bet were not binding. The dissolution of all contracts would not only ruin morality but spoil sport.

---

[25] From the 1662 Book of Common Prayer. The Old English meaning of "Prevent us" means "Go before us." "Prevent us, O Lord, in all our doings with thy most gracious favor, and further us with thy continual help; that in all our works, begun, continued, and ended in thee, we may glorify thy holy name, and finally by thy mercy obtain everlasting life; through Jesus Christ Our Lord."

Now betting and such sports are only the stunted and twisted shapes of the original instinct of man for adventure and romance, of which much has been said in these pages. And the perils, rewards, punishments, and fulfilments of an adventure must be real, or the adventure is only a shifting and heartless nightmare. If I bet I must be made to pay, or there is no poetry in betting. If I challenge I must be made to fight, or there is no poetry in challenging. If I vow to be faithful I must be cursed when I am unfaithful, or there is no fun in vowing. You could not even make a fairy tale from the experiences of a man who, when he was swallowed by a whale, might find himself at the top of the Eiffel Tower, or when he was turned into a frog might begin to behave like a flamingo. For the purpose even of the wildest romance results must be real; results must be irrevocable. Christian marriage is the great example of a real and irrevocable result; and that is why it is the chief subject and centre of all our romantic writing. And this is my last instance of the things that I should ask, and ask imperatively, of any social paradise; I should ask to be kept to my bargain, to have my oaths and engagements taken seriously; I should ask Utopia to avenge my honour on myself.

All my modern Utopian friends look at each other rather doubtfully, for their ultimate hope is the dissolution of all special ties. But again I seem to hear, like a kind of echo, an answer from beyond the world. "You will have real obligations, and therefore real adventures when you get to my Utopia. But the hardest obligation and the steepest adventure is to get there."

Chapter Summary

In this chapter Chesterton began by considering contemporary notions of progress in light of an ideal. The old idea of progress presupposed an ideal we were aspiring to reach; the new idea of progress means we can alter or change the ideal as much as we like. The new meaning, rather than leading to revolution or reform, leads to slavery. Without an ideal that is fixed, one that reflects the complexity of human need and the strange truth of the world, people are left with no means of truly changing themselves or the world. We stay the same because our vision of the future is always changing. In order to resolve this problem, Chesterton concluded (1) that we must have some sort of fixed ideal, (2) that this ideal must be a composite picture that holds different elements in proper proportion, and then (3) that this proportion implies that there must be an Artist or Designer behind it all. In each of these cases, Chesterton realized that Christianity showed up "with the exact answer that I required."

The latter part of the chapter turns to the question of Christianity and democracy. Why does Christianity, over against its critics, provide a more solid foundation for democracy? It comes from a realistic view of human nature and the fall—the way it lifts the humble, ordinary person while bringing low the rich and prideful. He closed the chapter with a discussion of the nature of love in its desire to bind itself.

Discussion Questions

1. What do you make of Chesterton's insistence on a "permanent ideal" as being necessary for true progress to be achieved?
2. What utopian dreams or ideals do we see on display in society today?
3. In what ways does Christianity provide a solid foundation for democracy over against aristocracy? How do Jesus's warnings to the rich affect our vision?

4. What do you think of Chesterton's linking of pride and a super-solemnity? How does humility help us take ourselves lightly?

EIGHT

In Chesterton's day, many religious leaders claimed the uniqueness of Christianity was not in its teaching on miracles or the divinity of Christ, but in its ethical stances and call for neighbor love. "The Romance of Orthodoxy" features Chesterton arguing for traditional Christianity against these liberalizing theologians, showing that it is precisely Christianity's traditional teaching that makes love for God and neighbor possible. At the end of chapter 6, Chesterton claimed there was nothing "so perilous or so exciting as orthodoxy," and now, in chapter 8, he shows us the "narrative romance" of Christianity as a story, as he contrasts orthodoxy with rival versions of Christianity that sink into dullness.

Chesterton's goal in this chapter is to make a case for some of the peculiar doctrines of Christianity that had become unpopular in his time. Against the assumption that the religions of the world are fundamentally equivalent, Chesterton shows how they differ significantly, especially in terms of looking inward or outward, or in distinguishing between God and the cosmos. "God is love" is the fact at the center of existence and is what gives rise to the romance of orthodoxy.

Memorable Parts to Look For

- Chesterton's case that people who seek freedom from orthodoxy fall into tyranny

- The difference in art depicting Christian saints and Buddhist monks
- Trinitarian doctrine as "this thing that bewilders the intellect" yet "utterly quiets the heart"
- Chesterton's riveting and intensely theological description of the paradox of Jesus in the garden and on the cross, the cry of God forsaken of God

The Romance of Orthodoxy

It is customary to complain of the bustle and strenuousness of our epoch. But in truth the chief mark of our epoch is a profound laziness and fatigue; and the fact is that the real laziness is the cause of the apparent bustle.

Take one quite external case; the streets are noisy with taxicabs and motorcars; but this is not due to human activity but to human repose. There would be less bustle if there were more activity, if people were simply walking about. Our world would be more silent if it were more strenuous.

And this which is true of the apparent physical bustle is true also of the apparent bustle of the intellect. Most of the machinery of modern language is labour-saving machinery; and it saves mental labour very much more than it ought. Scientific phrases are used like scientific wheels and piston rods to make swifter and smoother yet the path of the comfortable. Long words go rattling by us like long railway trains. We know they are carrying thousands who are too tired or too indolent to walk and think for themselves.

It is a good exercise to try for once in a way to express any opinion one holds in words of one syllable. If you say "The social utility of the indeterminate sentence is recognized by all criminologists as a part of our sociological evolution towards a more humane and scientific view of punishment," you can go on talking like that for hours with hardly a movement of the gray matter inside your skull. But if you begin "I wish Jones to go to gaol and Brown to say when Jones shall come out," you will discover, with a thrill of horror, that you are obliged to think. The long words are not the hard words; it is the short words that are hard. There is much more metaphysical subtlety in the word "damn" than in the word "degeneration."

The Meaning of "Liberal" When Applied to Theology

But these long comfortable words that save modern people the toil of reasoning have one particular aspect in which they are especially ruinous and confusing. This difficulty occurs when the same long word is used in different connections to mean quite different things. Thus, to take a well-known instance, the word "idealist" has one meaning as a piece of philosophy and quite another as a piece of moral rhetoric. In the same way the scientific materialists have had just reason to complain of people mixing up "materialist" as a term of cosmology with "materialist" as a moral taunt. So, to take a cheaper instance, the man who hates "progressives" in London always calls himself a "progressive" in South Africa.

A confusion quite as unmeaning as this has arisen in connection with the word "liberal" as applied to religion and as applied to politics and society. It is often suggested that all Liberals ought to be freethinkers, because they ought to love everything that is free. You might just as well say that all idealists ought to be High Churchmen, because they ought to love everything that is high. You might as well say that Low Churchmen ought to like Low Mass, or that Broad Churchmen ought to like broad jokes. The thing is a mere accident of words.

In actual modern Europe a freethinker does not mean a man who thinks for himself. It means a man who, having thought for himself, has come to one particular class of conclusions, the material origin of phenomena, the impossibility of miracles, the improbability of personal immortality and so on. And none of these ideas are particularly liberal. Nay, indeed almost all these ideas are definitely illiberal, as it is the purpose of this chapter to show.

The Illiberalism of Theological Liberalisers

In the few following pages I propose to point out as rapidly as possible that on every single one of the matters most strongly insisted on by liberalisers of theology their effect upon social practice would be definitely illiberal. Almost every contemporary proposal to bring freedom into the church is simply a proposal to bring tyranny into the world. For freeing the church now does not even mean freeing it in all directions. It means freeing that peculiar set of dogmas loosely called scientific, dogmas of monism,[1] of pantheism,[2] or of Arianism, or of necessity. And every one of these (and we will take them one by one) can be shown to be the natural ally of oppression. In fact, it is a remarkable circumstance (indeed not so very remarkable when one comes to think of it) that most things are the allies of oppression. There is only one thing that can never go past a certain point in its alliance with oppression—and that is orthodoxy. I may, it is true, twist orthodoxy so as partly to justify a tyrant. But I can easily make up a German philosophy to justify him entirely.

Now let us take in order the innovations that are the notes of the new theology or the modernist church. We concluded the last chapter with the discovery of one of them. The very doctrine which is called the most old-fashioned was found to be the only safeguard of the new democracies of the earth. The doctrine seemingly most unpopular was found to be the only strength of the people. In short,

---

[1] Monism is a theory or doctrine that denies the distinction between mind and matter or the world and God.

[2] Pantheism identifies God with the universe or sees the universe as a manifestation of God.

we found that the only logical negation of oligarchy was in the affirmation of original sin. So it is, I maintain, in all the other cases.

Materialism versus Miracles

I take the most obvious instance first, the case of miracles. For some extraordinary reason, there is a fixed notion that it is more liberal to disbelieve in miracles than to believe in them. Why, I cannot imagine, nor can anybody tell me. For some inconceivable cause a "broad" or "liberal" clergyman always means a man who wishes at least to diminish the number of miracles; it never means a man who wishes to increase that number. It always means a man who is free to disbelieve that Christ came out of His grave; it never means a man who is free to believe that his own aunt came out of her grave. It is common to find trouble in a parish because the parish priest cannot admit that St. Peter walked on water; yet how rarely do we find trouble in a parish because the clergyman says that his father walked on the Serpentine?[3]

And this is not because (as the swift secularist debater would immediately retort) miracles cannot be believed in our experience. It is not because "miracles do not happen," as in the dogma which Matthew Arnold recited with simple faith. More supernatural things are *alleged* to have happened in our time than would have been possible eighty years ago. Men of science believe in such marvels much more than they did: the most perplexing, and even horrible, prodigies of mind and spirit are always being unveiled in modern psychology. Things that the old science at least would frankly have rejected as miracles are hourly being asserted by the new science. The only thing which is still old-fashioned enough to reject miracles is the New Theology.

But in truth this notion that it is "free" to deny miracles has nothing to do with the evidence for or against them. It is a lifeless verbal prejudice of which the original life and beginning was not

[3] The Serpentine Lake in London's Kensington Gardens.

in the freedom of thought, but simply in the dogma of materialism. The man of the nineteenth century did not disbelieve in the Resurrection because his liberal Christianity allowed him to doubt it. He disbelieved in it because his very strict materialism did not allow him to believe it.

Tennyson, a very typical nineteenth century man, uttered one of the instinctive truisms of his contemporaries when he said that there was faith in their honest doubt.[4] There was indeed. Those words have a profound and even a horrible truth. In their doubt of miracles there was a faith in a fixed and godless fate; a deep and sincere faith in the incurable routine of the cosmos. The doubts of the agnostic were only the dogmas of the monist.

Of the fact and evidence of the supernatural I will speak afterwards. Here we are only concerned with this clear point; that insofar as the liberal idea of freedom can be said to be on either side in the discussion about miracles, it is obviously on the side of miracles. Reform or (in the only tolerable sense) progress means simply the gradual control of matter by mind. A miracle simply means the swift control of matter by mind.

If you wish to feed the people, you may think that feeding them miraculously in the wilderness is impossible—but you cannot think it illiberal. If you really want poor children to go to the seaside, you cannot think it illiberal that they should go there on flying dragons; you can only think it unlikely. A holiday, like Liberalism, only means the liberty of man. A miracle only means the liberty of God. You may conscientiously deny either of them, but you cannot call your denial a triumph of the liberal idea. The Catholic Church believed that man and God both had a sort of spiritual freedom. Calvinism took away the freedom from man, but left it to God. Scientific materialism binds the Creator Himself; it chains up God as the Apocalypse chained the devil.[5] It leaves nothing free in

---

[4] A reference to Alfred Lord Tennyson's *In Memoriam,* poem 96: "There lives more faith in honest doubt, / Believe me, than in half the creeds."

[5] A reference to Satan being bound in Revelation 20.

the universe. And those who assist this process are called the "liberal theologians."

This, as I say, is the lightest and most evident case. The assumption that there is something in the doubt of miracles akin to liberality or reform is literally the opposite of the truth. If a man cannot believe in miracles there is an end of the matter; he is not particularly liberal, but he is perfectly honourable and logical, which are much better things. But if he can believe in miracles, he is certainly the more liberal for doing so; because they mean first, the freedom of the soul, and secondly, its control over the tyranny of circumstance.

Sometimes this truth is ignored in a singularly naive way, even by the ablest men. For instance, Mr. Bernard Shaw speaks with hearty old-fashioned contempt for the idea of miracles, as if they were a sort of breach of faith on the part of nature: he seems strangely unconscious that miracles are only the final flowers of his own favourite tree, the doctrine of the omnipotence of will. Just in the same way he calls the desire for immortality a paltry selfishness, forgetting that he has just called the desire for life a healthy and heroic selfishness. How can it be noble to wish to make one's life infinite and yet mean to wish to make it immortal? No, if it is desirable that man should triumph over the cruelty of nature or custom, then miracles are certainly desirable; we will discuss afterwards whether they are possible.

Buddhism versus Christianity

But I must pass on to the larger cases of this curious error; the notion that the "liberalising" of religion in some way helps the liberation of the world. The second example of it can be found in the question of pantheism—or rather of a certain modern attitude which is often called immanentism, and which often is Buddhism. But this is so much more difficult a matter that I must approach it with rather more preparation.

The things said most confidently by advanced persons to crowded audiences are generally those quite opposite to the fact; it is actually our truisms that are untrue.

Here is a case. There is a phrase of facile liberality uttered again and again at ethical societies and parliaments of religion: "the religions of the earth differ in rites and forms, but they are the same in what they teach." It is false; it is the opposite of the fact. The religions of the earth do not greatly differ in rites and forms; they do greatly differ in what they teach. It is as if a man were to say, "Do not be misled by the fact that the *Church Times* and the *Freethinker* look utterly different, that one is painted on vellum and the other carved on marble, that one is triangular and the other hectagonal; read them and you will see that they say the same thing."[6]

The truth is, of course, that they are alike in everything except in the fact that they don't say the same thing. An atheist stockbroker in Surbiton looks exactly like a Swedenborgian stockbroker in Wimbledon.[7] You may walk round and round them and subject them to the most personal and offensive study without seeing anything Swedenborgian in the hat or anything particularly godless in the umbrella. It is exactly in their souls that they are divided. So the truth is that the difficulty of all the creeds of the earth is not as alleged in this cheap maxim: that they agree in meaning, but differ in machinery. It is exactly the opposite. They agree in machinery; almost every great religion on earth works with the same external methods, with priests, scriptures, altars, sworn brotherhoods, special feasts. They agree in the mode of teaching; what they differ about is the thing to be taught. Pagan optimists and Eastern pessimists

---

[6] *Church Times* is an independent Anglican weekly newspaper founded in 1863. The *Freethinker* is a British secular humanist magazine founded in 1881.

[7] Surbiton is a suburban neighborhood in southwest London. A Swedenborgian refers to a follower of Emmanuel Swedenborg (1688–1772) who claimed divine revelation for his reinterpretation of the Scriptures. Wimbledon is part of Greater London.

would both have temples, just as Liberals and Tories would both have newspapers. Creeds that exist to destroy each other both have scriptures, just as armies that exist to destroy each other both have guns.

The great example of this alleged identity of all human religions is the alleged spiritual identity of Buddhism and Christianity. Those who adopt this theory generally avoid the ethics of most other creeds, except, indeed, Confucianism, which they like because it is not a creed.[8] But they are cautious in their praises of Mahommedanism,[9] generally confining themselves to imposing its morality only upon the refreshment of the lower classes. They seldom suggest the Mahommedan view of marriage (for which there is a great deal to be said), and towards Thugs and fetish worshippers their attitude may even be called cold. But in the case of the great religion of Gautama they feel sincerely a similarity.[10]

Students of popular science, like Mr. Blatchford, are always insisting that Christianity and Buddhism are very much alike, especially Buddhism. This is generally believed, and I believed it myself until I read a book giving the reasons for it. The reasons were of two kinds: resemblances that meant nothing because they were common to all humanity, and resemblances which were not resemblances at all. The author solemnly explained that the two creeds were alike in things in which all creeds are alike, or else he described them as alike in some point in which they are quite obviously different.

Thus, as a case of the first class, he said that both Christ and Buddha were called by the divine voice coming out of the sky, as if you would expect the divine voice to come out of the coal cellar.

---

[8] Confucianism is a system of philosophical and ethical teachings, also known as Ruism, which originated in ancient China.

[9] Islam. Chesterton refers to Islam as "Mahommedanism," in relation to the chief prophet of Islam, Muhammad.

[10] Gautama Buddha—the philosopher and religious leader from ancient India (fifth to fourth century BC), revered as the founder of Buddhism.

Or, again, it was gravely urged that these two Eastern teachers, by a singular coincidence, both had to do with the washing of feet. You might as well say that it was a remarkable coincidence that they both had feet to wash.

And the other class of similarities were those which simply were not similar. Thus this reconciler of the two religions draws earnest attention to the fact that at certain religious feasts the robe of the Lama is rent in pieces out of respect, and the remnants highly valued. But this is the reverse of a resemblance, for the garments of Christ were not rent in pieces out of respect, but out of derision; and the remnants were not highly valued except for what they would fetch in the rag shops. It is rather like alluding to the obvious connection between the two ceremonies of the sword: when it taps a man's shoulder, and when it cuts off his head. It is not at all similar for the man.

These scraps of puerile pedantry would indeed matter little if it were not also true that the alleged philosophical resemblances are also of these two kinds, either proving too much or not proving anything. That Buddhism approves of mercy or of self-restraint is not to say that it is specially like Christianity; it is only to say that it is not utterly unlike all human existence. Buddhists disapprove in theory of cruelty or excess because all sane human beings disapprove in theory of cruelty or excess. But to say that Buddhism and Christianity give the same philosophy of these things is simply false. All humanity does agree that we are in a net of sin. Most of humanity agrees that there is some way out. But as to what is the way out, I do not think that there are two institutions in the universe which contradict each other so flatly as Buddhism and Christianity.

Even when I thought, with most other well-informed, though unscholarly, people, that Buddhism and Christianity were alike, there was one thing about them that always perplexed me; I mean the startling difference in their type of religious art. I do not mean in its technical style of representation, but in the things that it was manifestly meant to represent. No two ideals could be more opposite than a Christian saint in a Gothic cathedral and a Buddhist saint in a Chinese temple. The opposition exists at every point; but perhaps the shortest statement of it is that the Buddhist saint always has his eyes shut, while the Christian saint always has them very wide open. The Buddhist saint has a sleek and harmonious body, but his eyes are heavy and sealed with sleep. The mediaeval saint's body is wasted to its crazy bones, but his eyes are frightfully alive. There cannot be any real community of spirit between forces that produced symbols so different as that. Granted that both images are extravagances, are perversions of the pure creed, it must be a real divergence which could produce such opposite extravagances. The Buddhist is looking with a peculiar intentness inwards. The Christian is staring with a frantic intentness outwards. If we follow that clue steadily we shall find some interesting things.

"The Universal Self" versus Individuality

A short time ago Mrs. Besant,[11] in an interesting essay, announced that there was only one religion in the world, that all faiths were only versions or perversions of it, and that she was quite prepared to say what it was. According to Mrs. Besant this universal Church is simply the universal self. It is the doctrine that we are really all one person; that there are no real walls of individuality between man and man. If I may put it so, she does not tell us to love our neighbours; she tells us to be our neighbours. That is Mrs. Besant's thoughtful and suggestive description of the religion in which all men must find themselves in agreement. And I never heard of any suggestion in my life with which I more violently disagree. I want to love my neighbour not because he is I, but precisely because he is not I. I want to adore the world, not as one likes a looking-glass,

[11] Annie Besant (1847–1933) was a British socialist and writer who joined the Theosophical Society—a movement that sought to reconcile all religions, founded by Madame Blavatsky in 1875. Besant was president of the society at the time Chesterton wrote *Orthodoxy*.

because it is one's self, but as one loves a woman, because she is entirely different.

If souls are separate, love is possible. If souls are united, love is obviously impossible. A man may be said loosely to love himself, but he can hardly fall in love with himself, or, if he does, it must be a monotonous courtship. If the world is full of real selves, they can be really unselfish selves. But upon Mrs. Besant's principle the whole cosmos is only one enormously selfish person.

It is just here that Buddhism is on the side of modern pantheism and immanence. And it is just here that Christianity is on the side of humanity and liberty and love. Love desires personality; therefore love desires division. It is the instinct of Christianity to be glad that God has broken the universe into little pieces, because they are living pieces. It is her instinct to say "little children, love one another"[12] rather than to tell one large person to love himself.

This is the intellectual abyss between Buddhism and Christianity; that for the Buddhist or Theosophist personality is the fall of man, for the Christian it is the purpose of God, the whole point of his cosmic idea. The world-soul of the Theosophists asks man to love it only in order that man may throw himself into it. But the divine centre of Christianity actually threw man out of it in order that he might love it. The oriental deity is like a giant who should have lost his leg or hand and be always seeking to find it; but the Christian power is like some giant who in a strange generosity should cut off his right hand, so that it might of its own accord shake hands with him.

We come back to the same tireless note touching the nature of Christianity; all modern philosophies are chains which connect and fetter; Christianity is a sword which separates and sets free. No other philosophy makes God actually rejoice in the separation of the universe into living souls. But according to orthodox Christianity this separation between God and man is sacred, because this is eternal. That a man may love God it is necessary that there should be not only a God to be loved, but a man to love him.

[12] Chesterton's rendering of 1 John 4:7.

All those vague theosophical minds for whom the universe is an immense melting-pot are exactly the minds which shrink instinctively from that earthquake saying of our Gospels, which declare that the Son of God came not with peace but with a sundering sword.[13] The saying rings entirely true even considered as what it obviously is; the statement that any man who preaches real love is bound to beget hate. It is as true of democratic fraternity as a divine love; sham love ends in compromise and common philosophy; but real love has always ended in bloodshed. Yet there is another and yet more awful truth behind the obvious meaning of this utterance of our Lord. According to Himself the Son was a sword separating brother and brother that they should for an aeon hate each other. But the Father also was a sword, which in the black beginning separated brother and brother, so that they should love each other at last.

This is the meaning of that almost insane happiness in the eyes of the mediaeval saint in the picture. This is the meaning of the sealed eyes of the superb Buddhist image. The Christian saint is happy because he has verily been cut off from the world; he is separate from things and is staring at them in astonishment. But why should the Buddhist saint be astonished at things?—since there is really only one thing, and that being impersonal can hardly be astonished at itself. There have been many pantheist poems suggesting wonder, but no really successful ones. The pantheist cannot wonder, for he cannot praise God or praise anything as really distinct from himself.

Individuality's Effect on Ethics

Our immediate business here, however, is with the effect of this Christian admiration (which strikes outwards, towards a deity distinct from the worshipper) upon the general need for ethical activity and social reform. And surely its effect is sufficiently obvious.

[13] Matt 10:34.

There is no real possibility of getting out of pantheism, any special impulse to moral action. For pantheism implies in its nature that one thing is as good as another; whereas action implies in its nature that one thing is greatly preferable to another.

Swinburne in the high summer of his scepticism tried in vain to wrestle with this difficulty. In "Songs before Sunrise," written under the inspiration of Garibaldi and the revolt of Italy he proclaimed the newer religion and the purer God which should wither up all the priests of the world:[14]

> *"What dost thou now*
> *Looking Godward to cry*
> *I am I, thou art thou,*
> *I am low, thou art high,*
> *I am thou that thou seekest to find him, find*
> *thou but thyself, thou art I."*[15]

Of which the immediate and evident deduction is that tyrants are as much the sons of God as Garibaldis; and that King Bomba of Naples having, with the utmost success, "found himself" is identical with the ultimate good in all things.[16] The truth is that the western energy that dethrones tyrants has been directly due to the western theology that says "I am I, thou art thou." The same spiritual separation which looked up and saw a good king in the universe looked up and saw a bad king in Naples. The worshippers of Bomba's god dethroned Bomba. The worshippers of Swinburne's god have covered Asia for centuries and have never dethroned a tyrant. The Indian saint may reasonably shut his eyes because he

---

[14] Giuseppe Garibaldi (1807–82) was an Italian general and patriot who contributed to the unification and creation of the kingdom of Italy.

[15] From "Hertha" by Charles Swinburne.

[16] "Bomba" was an epithet given to Ferdinand II (1810–59), king of the two Sicilies when revolution broke out in Sicily in 1848, because he subdued the country by bombing its main cities and killing many civilians, even after they had surrendered.

is looking at that which is I and Thou and We and They and It. It is a rational occupation: but it is not true in theory and not true in fact that it helps the Indian to keep an eye on Lord Curzon.[17] That external vigilance which has always been the mark of Christianity (the command that we should *watch* and pray[18]) has expressed itself both in typical western orthodoxy and in typical western politics: but both depend on the idea of a divinity transcendent, different from ourselves, a deity that disappears. Certainly the most sagacious creeds may suggest that we should pursue God into deeper and deeper rings of the labyrinth of our own ego. But only we of Christendom have said that we should hunt God like an eagle upon the mountains: and we have killed all monsters in the chase.

Here again, therefore, we find that insofar as we value democracy and the self-renewing energies of the west, we are much more likely to find them in the old theology than the new. If we want reform, we must adhere to orthodoxy: especially in this matter (so much disputed in the counsels of Mr. R. J. Campbell), the matter of insisting on the immanent or the transcendent deity. By insisting specially on the immanence of God we get introspection, self-isolation, quietism, social indifference—Tibet.[19] By insisting specially on the transcendence of God we get wonder, curiosity, moral and political adventure, righteous indignation—Christendom. Insisting that God is inside man, man is always inside himself. By insisting that God transcends man, man has transcended himself.

Unitarianism versus Trinitarian Doctrine

If we take any other doctrine that has been called old-fashioned we shall find the case the same. It is the same, for instance, in the deep matter of the Trinity. Unitarians (a sect never to be mentioned

[17] Lord George Curzon (1859–1925) was viceroy and governor-general of India from 1898 to 1905.

[18] Matt 26:41.

[19] Tibet is a region in east Asia, home to Tibetan Buddhism.

without a special respect for their distinguished intellectual dignity and high intellectual honour) are often reformers by the accident that throws so many small sects into such an attitude.[20] But there is nothing in the least liberal or akin to reform in the substitution of pure monotheism for the Trinity. The complex God of the Athanasian Creed may be an enigma for the intellect;[21] but He is far less likely to gather the mystery and cruelty of a Sultan than the lonely god of Omar or Mahomet.[22] The god who is a mere awful unity is not only a king but an Eastern king.

The *heart* of humanity, especially of European humanity, is certainly much more satisfied by the strange hints and symbols that gather round the Trinitarian idea, the image of a council at which mercy pleads as well as justice, the conception of a sort of liberty and variety existing even in the inmost chamber of the world. For Western religion has always felt keenly the idea "it is not well for man to be alone."[23] The social instinct asserted itself everywhere as when the Eastern idea of hermits was practically expelled by the Western idea of monks. So even asceticism became brotherly; and the Trappists were sociable even when they were silent.[24]

If this love of a living complexity be our test, it is certainly healthier to have the Trinitarian religion than the Unitarian. For to us Trinitarians (if I may say it with reverence)—to us God Himself is a society. It is indeed a fathomless mystery of theology, and even if I were theologian enough to deal with it directly, it would not be

---

[20] Unitarians believe God is one person, rather than a Trinity. Chesterton's parents were Unitarians and "freethinkers" who nevertheless baptized Chesterton as an infant in the Church of England.

[21] The Athanasian Creed was a sixth-century creedal statement of Christianity that focused on Trinitarian doctrine and Christology.

[22] Omar was a senior companion of the Islamic prophet Muhammad. Mahomet is an alternate spelling for Muhammad.

[23] Chesterton's rendering of Gen 2:18.

[24] The Trappists are formal members of the Order of Cistercians of the Strict Observance, a Catholic religious order that branched off from the Cistercian monks.

relevant to do so here. Suffice it to say here that this triple enigma is as comforting as wine and open as an English fireside; that this thing that bewilders the intellect utterly quiets the heart: but out of the desert, from the dry places and the dreadful suns, come the cruel children of the lonely God; the real Unitarians who with scimitar in hand have laid waste the world. For it is not well for God to be alone.

Fatalism versus Freedom of the Will

Again, the same is true of that difficult matter of the danger of the soul, which has unsettled so many just minds. To hope for all souls is imperative; and it is quite tenable that their salvation is inevitable. It is tenable, but it is not specially favourable to activity or progress. Our fighting and creative society ought rather to insist on the danger of everybody, on the fact that every man is hanging by a thread or clinging to a precipice. To say that all will be well anyhow is a comprehensible remark: but it cannot be called the blast of a trumpet. Europe ought rather to emphasize possible perdition; and Europe always has emphasized it. Here its highest religion is at one with all its cheapest romances.

To the Buddhist or the eastern fatalist, existence is a science or a plan, which must end up in a certain way. But to a Christian existence is a *story*, which may end up in any way. In a thrilling novel (that purely Christian product) the hero is not eaten by cannibals; but it is essential to the existence of the thrill that he *might* be eaten by cannibals. The hero must (so to speak) be an eatable hero. So Christian morals have always said to the man, not that he would lose his soul, but that he must take care that he didn't. In Christian morals, in short, it is wicked to call a man "damned": but it is strictly religious and philosophic to call him damnable.

All Christianity concentrates on the man at the crossroads. The vast and shallow philosophies, the huge syntheses of humbug, all talk about ages and evolution and ultimate developments. The true philosophy is concerned with the instant. Will a man take this road or that?—that is the only thing to think about, if you enjoy thinking. The aeons are easy enough to think about, any one can think about them. The instant is really awful: and it is because our religion has intensely felt the instant, that it has in literature dealt much with battle and in theology dealt much with hell. It is full of *danger*, like a boy's book: it is at an immortal crisis.

There is a great deal of real similarity between popular fiction and the religion of the western people. If you say that popular fiction is vulgar and tawdry, you only say what the dreary and well-informed say also about the images in the Catholic churches. Life (according to the faith) is very like a serial story in a magazine: life ends with the promise (or menace) "to be continued in our next." Also, with a noble vulgarity, life imitates the serial and leaves off at the exciting moment. For death is distinctly an exciting moment.

But the point is that a story is exciting because it has in it so strong an element of will, of what theology calls free will. You cannot finish a sum how you like. But you can finish a story how you like. When somebody discovered the Differential Calculus there was only one Differential Calculus he could discover. But when Shakespeare killed Romeo he might have married him to Juliet's old nurse if he had felt inclined. And Christendom has excelled in the narrative romance exactly because it has insisted on the theological free will.

It is a large matter and too much to one side of the road to be discussed adequately here; but this is the real objection to that torrent of modern talk about treating crime as disease, about making a prison merely a hygienic environment like a hospital, of healing sin by slow scientific methods. The fallacy of the whole thing is that evil is a matter of active choice whereas disease is not. If you say that you are going to cure a profligate as you cure an asthmatic, my cheap and obvious answer is, "Produce the people who want to be asthmatics as many people want to be profligates." A man may lie still and be cured of a malady. But he must not lie still if he wants to be cured of a sin; on the contrary, he must get up and jump about violently. The whole point indeed is perfectly expressed in the very word which we use for a man in hospital; "patient" is in the passive mood; "sinner" is in the active. If a man is to be saved from influenza, he may be a patient. But if he is to be saved from forging, he must be not a patient but an *impatient*. He must be personally impatient with forgery. All moral reform must start in the active not the passive will.

Here again we reach the same substantial conclusion. Insofar as we desire the definite reconstructions and the dangerous revolutions which have distinguished European civilization, we shall not discourage the thought of possible ruin; we shall rather encourage it. If we want, like the Eastern saints, merely to contemplate how right things are, of course we shall only say that they must go right. But if we particularly want to *make* them go right, we must insist that they may go wrong.

Arianism versus the Divinity of Christ

Lastly, this truth is yet again true in the case of the common modern attempts to diminish or to explain away the divinity of Christ. The thing may be true or not; that I shall deal with before I end. But if the divinity is true it is certainly terribly revolutionary. That a good man may have his back to the wall is no more than we knew already; but that God could have his back to the wall is a boast for all insurgents forever. Christianity is the only religion on earth that has felt that omnipotence made God incomplete. Christianity alone has felt that God, to be wholly God, must have been a rebel as well as a king. Alone of all creeds, Christianity has added courage to the virtues of the Creator. For the only courage worth calling courage must necessarily mean that the soul passes a breaking point—and does not break.

In this indeed I approach a matter more dark and awful than it is easy to discuss; and I apologise in advance if any of my phrases fall wrong or seem irreverent touching a matter which the greatest saints and thinkers have justly feared to approach. But in that terrific tale of the Passion there is a distinct emotional suggestion that the author of all things (in some unthinkable way) went not only through agony, but through doubt. It is written, "Thou shalt not tempt the Lord thy God."[25] No; but the Lord thy God may tempt Himself; and it seems as if this was what happened in Gethsemane. In a garden Satan tempted man: and in a garden God tempted God. He passed in some superhuman manner through our human horror of pessimism. When the world shook and the sun was wiped out of heaven, it was not at the crucifixion, but at the cry from the cross: the cry which confessed that God was forsaken of God.

And now let the revolutionists choose a creed from all the creeds and a god from all the gods of the world, carefully weighing all the gods of inevitable recurrence and of unalterable power. They will not find another god who has himself been in revolt. Nay, (the matter grows too difficult for human speech,) but let the atheists themselves choose a god. They will find only one divinity who ever uttered their isolation; only one religion in which God seemed for an instant to be an atheist.

Orthodoxy as the Fountain of Revolution and Reform

These can be called the essentials of the old orthodoxy, of which the chief merit is that it is the natural fountain of revolution and reform; and of which the chief defect is that it is obviously only an abstract assertion. Its main advantage is that it is the most adventurous and manly of all theologies. Its chief disadvantage is simply that it is a theology. It can always be urged against it that it is in its nature arbitrary and in the air. But it is not so high in the air but that great archers spend their whole lives in shooting arrows at it—yes, and their last arrows; there are men who will ruin themselves and ruin their civilization if they may ruin also this old fantastic tale.

This is the last and most astounding fact about this faith; that its enemies will use any weapon against it, the swords that cut their

[25] Matt 4:7.

own fingers, and the firebrands that burn their own homes. Men who begin to fight the Church for the sake of freedom and humanity end by flinging away freedom and humanity if only they may fight the Church. This is no exaggeration; I could fill a book with the instances of it.

Mr. Blatchford set out, as an ordinary Bible-smasher, to prove that Adam was guiltless of sin against God; in maneuvering so as to maintain this he admitted, as a mere side issue, that all the tyrants, from Nero to King Leopold,[26] were guiltless of any sin against humanity. I know a man who has such a passion for proving that he will have no personal existence after death that he falls back on the position that he has no personal existence now. He invokes Buddhism and says that all souls fade into each other; in order to prove that he cannot go to heaven he proves that he cannot go to Hartlepool.[27] I have known people who protested against religious education with arguments against any education, saying that the child's mind must grow freely or that the old must not teach the young. I have known people who showed that there could be no divine judgment by showing that there can be no human judgment, even for practical purposes. They burned their own corn to set fire to the church; they smashed their own tools to smash it; any stick was good enough to beat it with, though it were the last stick of their own dismembered furniture.

We do not admire, we hardly excuse, the fanatic who wrecks this world for love of the other. But what are we to say of the fanatic who wrecks this world out of hatred of the other? He sacrifices the very existence of humanity to the non-existence of God. He offers his victims not to the altar, but merely to assert the idleness of the altar and the emptiness of the throne. He is ready to ruin even that primary ethic by which all things live, for his strange and eternal vengeance upon someone who never lived at all.

---

[26] Leopold II (1835–1909), king of the Belgians, was notorious for his exploitation of the region of Congo and barbaric treatment of the natives.

[27] A town in County Durham, England.

And yet the thing hangs in the heavens unhurt. Its opponents only succeed in destroying all that they themselves justly hold dear. They do not destroy orthodoxy; they only destroy political and common courage sense. They do not prove that Adam was not responsible to God; how could they prove it? They only prove (from their premises) that the Czar is not responsible to Russia. They do not prove that Adam should not have been punished by God; they only prove that the nearest sweater should not be punished by men. With their oriental doubts about personality they do not make certain that we shall have no personal life hereafter; they only make certain that we shall not have a very jolly or complete one here. With their paralysing hints of all conclusions coming out wrong they do not tear the book of the Recording Angel; they only make it a little harder to keep the books of Marshall & Snelgrove.[28]

Not only is the faith the mother of all worldly energies, but its foes are the fathers of all worldly confusion. The secularists have not wrecked divine things; but the secularists have wrecked secular things, if that is any comfort to them. The Titans did not scale heaven; but they laid waste the world.

---

[28] A large department store in London founded in 1837, now part of Debenhams.

Chapter Summary

In this chapter Chesterton took on the meaning of the words "liberal" and "freedom" in his day, in order to show that those who would claim to be "freethinkers" in relation to theology or "broad" minded and "liberal" in their approach to Christian doctrine actually disregard the orthodox teaching that *secures* freedom of thought and liberality in all sorts of areas. For example, the materialist who is seen as "liberal" in his approach to miracles (that is, he denies them all) is beholden to his dogma against miracles and is in no real sense *free* to believe in any of them, whereas the Christian who is orthodox is free to believe *or* disbelieve miracle stories, based on evidence.

Chesterton showed how pantheism, expressed primarily here through the example of Buddhism, removes any distinction between the Creator and the creation, which leaves us without the freedom to reform. Likewise, by making God and the universe one, we lose the individuality of persons and the freedom to *love*. This problem, Chesterton pointed out, is the same with the Unitarian and Islamic understanding of God over against the communion present in orthodoxy's teaching of God as a Trinity. Furthermore, the universalist idea that our choices have no bearing on our eternal destiny takes the drama out of life and leaves us with a fatalistic view of the world in which people have no freedom to take part in changing their lives. Finally, Chesterton contrasted the diminishment of Christ's divinity with a riveting portrait of drama in which Christ, through His passion, opens the way to victory.

Discussion Questions

1. How do you respond to the idea that the major religions are basically the same?
2. Why is the truth of the Trinity necessary in order to say "God is love"?

3. In what ways does Christianity lead us out of the inner depths of our hearts and open our eyes to the world around us?
4. In what ways do people downplay or diminish the divinity of Christ today?

NINE

In this final chapter, Chesterton begins with a question: would it be possible to take all of these discoveries, hold onto the central insights, and yet dismiss Christian doctrine? Can we take the truths we find in orthodoxy but then advance beyond Christianity? In response, we see Chesterton reinforcing the link between the common-sense truths he's discovered and the worldview of Christianity. Without a supernatural authority (like the church) to protect even what we discover in nature, what we see in nature loses its glory.

Chesterton's goal in this chapter is to demonstrate the trustworthiness of the Christian church in its outlook on life. By questioning the "facts" of those who criticize Christianity, and by examining the accumulation of evidence brought by Christians and propounded by the church, Chesterton seeks to show why it is reasonable to believe the Christian creed. No matter what we believe, we take it on someone's authority. The adventure of faith within the boundaries of authority (in this case, the authority of Christianity) is what protects the romance we most desire in life.

Memorable Parts to Look For

- Chesterton's portrait of Jesus Christ, intended to startle our imagination into seeing him as if for the first time
- Chesterton's description of the living church over against the great thinkers of old

- Chesterton's case for miracles
- Joy as the "gigantic secret of the Christian"
- The surprising final few sentences of this book

AUTHORITY AND THE ADVENTURER

The last chapter has been concerned with the contention that orthodoxy is not only (as is often urged) the only safe guardian of morality or order, but is also the only logical guardian of liberty, innovation and advance. If we wish to pull down the prosperous oppressor we cannot do it with the new doctrine of human perfectibility; we can do it with the old doctrine of Original Sin. If we want to uproot inherent cruelties or lift up lost populations we cannot do it with the scientific theory that matter precedes mind; we can do it with the supernatural theory that mind precedes matter. If we wish specially to awaken people to social vigilance and tireless pursuit of practise, we cannot help it much by insisting on the Immanent God and the Inner Light: for these are at best reasons for contentment; we can help it much by insisting on the transcendent God and the flying and escaping gleam; for that means divine discontent. If we wish particularly to assert the idea of a generous balance against that of a dreadful autocracy we shall instinctively be Trinitarian rather than Unitarian. If we desire European civilization to be a raid and a rescue, we shall insist rather that souls are in real peril than that their peril is ultimately unreal. And if we wish to exalt the outcast and the crucified, we shall rather wish to think that a veritable God was crucified, rather than a mere sage or hero. Above all, if we wish to protect the poor we shall be in favour of fixed rules and clear dogmas. The *rules* of a club are occasionally in favour of the poor member. The drift of a club is always in favour of the rich one.

The Crucial Question: Truths without Doctrines

And now we come to the crucial question which truly concludes the whole matter. A reasonable agnostic, if he has happened to agree with me so far, may justly turn round and say, "You have found a practical philosophy in the doctrine of the Fall; very well. You have found a side of democracy now dangerously neglected wisely asserted in Original Sin; all right. You have found a truth in the doctrine of hell; I congratulate you. You are convinced that worshippers of a personal God look outwards and are progressive; I congratulate them. But even supposing that those doctrines do include those truths, why cannot you take the truths and leave the doctrines? Granted that all modern society is trusting the rich too much because it does not allow for human weakness; granted that orthodox ages have had a great advantage because (believing in the Fall) they did allow for human weakness, why cannot you simply allow for human weakness without believing in the Fall? If you have discovered that the idea of damnation represents a healthy idea of danger, why can you not simply take the idea of danger and leave the idea of damnation? If you see clearly the kernel of common sense in the nut of Christian orthodoxy, why cannot you simply take the kernel and leave the nut? Why cannot you (to use that cant phrase of the newspapers which I, as a highly scholarly agnostic, am a little ashamed of using) why cannot you simply take what is good in Christianity, what you can define as valuable, what you can comprehend, and leave all the rest, all the absolute dogmas that are in their nature incomprehensible?"

This is the real question; this is the last question; and it is a pleasure to try to answer it.

The First Answer: The Evidence Points to Its Truth

The first answer is simply to say that I am a rationalist. I like to have some intellectual justification for my intuitions. If I am treating man as a fallen being it is an intellectual convenience to me to believe that he fell; and I find, for some odd psychological reason, that I can deal better with a man's exercise of freewill if I believe that he has got it.

But I am in this matter yet more definitely a rationalist. I do not propose to turn this book into one of ordinary Christian apologetics; I should be glad to meet at any other time the enemies of Christianity in that more obvious arena. Here I am only giving an account of my own growth in spiritual certainty. But I may pause to remark that the more I saw of the merely abstract arguments against the Christian cosmology, the less I thought of them. I mean that having found the moral atmosphere of the Incarnation to be common sense, I then looked at the established intellectual arguments against the Incarnation and found them to be common nonsense. In case the argument should be thought to suffer from the absence of the ordinary apologetic I will here very briefly summarise my own arguments and conclusions on the purely objective or scientific truth of the matter.

If I am asked, as a purely intellectual question, why I believe in Christianity, I can only answer, "For the same reason that an intelligent agnostic disbelieves in Christianity." I believe in it quite rationally upon the evidence.

But the evidence in my case, as in that of the intelligent agnostic, is not really in this or that alleged demonstration; it is in an enormous accumulation of small but unanimous facts. The secularist is not to be blamed because his objections to Christianity are miscellaneous and even scrappy; it is precisely such scrappy evidence that does convince the mind. I mean that a man may well be less convinced of a philosophy from four books, than from one book, one battle, one landscape, and one old friend. The very fact that the things are of different kinds increases the importance of the fact that they all point to one conclusion. Now, the non-Christianity of the average educated man today is almost always, to do him justice, made up of these loose but living experiences. I can only say that my evidences for Christianity are of the same vivid but varied kind as his evidences against it. For when I look at these various anti-Christian truths, I simply discover that none of them are true. I discover that the true tide and force of all the facts flows the other way.

Considering Three Objections

Let us take cases. Many a sensible modern man must have abandoned Christianity under the pressure of three such converging convictions as these:

(1) first, that men, with their shape, structure, and sexuality, are, after all, very much like beasts, a mere variety of the animal kingdom;

(2) second, that primeval religion arose in ignorance and fear;

(3) third, that priests have blighted societies with bitterness and gloom.

Those three anti-Christian arguments are very different; but they are all quite logical and legitimate; and they all converge. The only objection to them (I discover) is that they are all untrue.

Man Is Like the Beasts

If you leave off looking at books about beasts and men, if you begin to look at beasts and men then (if you have any humour or imagination, any sense of the frantic or the farcical) you will observe that the startling thing is not how like man is to the brutes, but how unlike he is. It is the monstrous scale of his divergence that requires an explanation.

That man and brute are like is, in a sense, a truism; but that being so like they should then be so insanely unlike, that is the shock and the enigma. That an ape has hands is far less interesting to the philosopher than the fact that having hands he does next to nothing with them; does not play knuckle-bones or the violin; does not carve marble or carve mutton. People talk of barbaric architecture and debased art. But elephants do not build colossal temples of ivory even in a rococo style; camels do not paint even bad pictures, though equipped with the material of many camel's-hair brushes. Certain modern dreamers say that ants and bees have a society superior to ours. They have, indeed, a civilization; but that very truth only reminds us that it is an inferior civilization. Who ever found an anthill decorated with the statues of celebrated ants? Who has seen a beehive carved with the images of gorgeous queens of old?

No; the chasm between man and other creatures may have a natural explanation, but it is a chasm. We talk of wild animals; but man is the only wild animal. It is man that has broken out. All other animals are tame animals; following the rugged respectability of the tribe or type. All other animals are domestic animals; man alone is ever undomestic, either as a profligate or a monk. So that this first superficial reason for materialism is, if anything, a reason for its opposite; it is exactly where biology leaves off that all religion begins.

Primeval Religion Is in Darkness and Terror

It would be the same if I examined the second of the three chance rationalist arguments; the argument that all that we call divine began in some darkness and terror. When I did attempt to examine the foundations of this modern idea I simply found that there were none.

Science knows nothing whatever about prehistoric man; for the excellent reason that he is prehistoric. A few professors choose to conjecture that such things as human sacrifice were once innocent and general and that they gradually dwindled; but there is no direct evidence of it, and the small amount of indirect evidence is very much the other way. In the earliest legends we have, such as the tales of Isaac and of Iphigenia,[1] human sacrifice is not introduced as something old, but rather as something new; as a strange and frightful exception darkly demanded by the gods. History says nothing; and legends all say that the earth was kinder in its earliest time. There is no tradition of progress; but the whole human race has a tradition of the Fall. Amusingly enough, indeed, the very dissemination of this idea is used against its authenticity. Learned men literally say that this pre-historic calamity cannot be true because every race of mankind remembers it. I cannot keep pace with these paradoxes.

Priests Darken the World

And if we took the third chance instance, it would be the same; the view that priests darken and embitter the world. I look at the world and simply discover that they don't.

Those countries in Europe which are still influenced by priests, are exactly the countries where there is still singing and dancing and coloured dresses and art in the open air. Catholic doctrine and discipline may be walls; but they are the walls of a playground. Christianity is the only frame which has preserved the pleasure of Paganism.

We might fancy some children playing on the flat grassy top of some tall island in the sea. So long as there was a wall round the cliff's edge they could fling themselves into every frantic game and make the place the noisiest of nurseries. But the walls were knocked down, leaving the naked peril of the precipice. They did not fall over; but when their friends returned to them they were all huddled in terror in the centre of the island; and their song had ceased.

---

[1] Isaac refers to the story of Abraham's call to sacrifice him, as told in Genesis 22. Iphigenia refers to the daughter of King Agamemnon in Greek mythology, who is required by the goddess Artemis to be sacrificed due to Agamemnon's accidental killing of one of Artemis's sacred deer.

Turning Around the Objections

Thus these three facts of experience, such facts as go to make an agnostic, are, in this view, turned totally round. I am left saying, "Give me an explanation, first, of the towering eccentricity of man among the brutes; second, of the vast human tradition of some ancient happiness; third, of the partial perpetuation of such pagan joy in the countries of the Catholic Church."

One explanation, at any rate, covers all three: the theory that twice was the natural order interrupted by some explosion or revelation such as people now call "psychic." Once Heaven came upon the earth with a power or seal called the image of God, whereby man took command of Nature; and once again (when in empire after empire men had been found wanting) Heaven came to save mankind in the awful shape of a man. This would explain why the mass of men always look backwards; and why the only corner where they in any sense look forwards is the little continent where Christ has His Church.

I know it will be said that Japan has become progressive. But how can this be an answer when even in saying "Japan has become progressive," we really only mean, "Japan has become European"?

But I wish here not so much to insist on my own explanation as to insist on my original remark. I agree with the ordinary unbelieving man in the street in being guided by three or four odd facts all pointing to something; only when I came to look at the facts I always found they pointed to something else.

Considering Three More Objections

I have given an imaginary triad of such ordinary anti-Christian arguments; if that be too narrow a basis I will give on the spur of the moment another. These are the kind of thoughts which in combination create the impression that Christianity is something weak and diseased.

(1) First, for instance, that Jesus was a gentle creature, sheepish and unworldly, a mere ineffectual appeal to the world;

(2) second, that Christianity arose and flourished in the dark ages of ignorance, and that to these the Church would drag us back;

(3) third, that the people still strongly religious or (if you will) superstitious—such people as the Irish—are weak, unpractical, and behind the times.

I only mention these ideas to affirm the same thing: that when I looked into them independently I found, not that the conclusions were unphilosophical, but simply that the facts were not facts.

Christ the Weakling

Instead of looking at books and pictures about the New Testament, I looked at the New Testament. There I found an account, not in the least of a person with his hair parted in the middle or his hands clasped in appeal, but of an extraordinary being with lips of thunder and acts of lurid decision, flinging down tables, casting out devils, passing with the wild secrecy of the wind from mountain isolation to a sort of dreadful demagogy; a being who often acted like an angry god—and always like a god. Christ had even a literary style of his own, not to be found, I think, elsewhere; it consists of an almost furious use of the *a fortiori*.[2] His "how much more" is piled one upon another like castle upon castle in the clouds.[3]

The diction used *about* Christ has been, and perhaps wisely, sweet and submissive. But the diction used by Christ is quite

---

[2] Latin, literally "from the stronger." In legal writing, the term is used in English within the context of "from the stronger argument." If one fact is true, then one can assume a second fact is true.

[3] "How much more" is a common phrase found throughout Jesus's teachings, this is an example of the *a fortiori* literary form, a rhetorical device that compares two things and concludes that if the *first* thing is true, the *second* must be even more so. "If then God so clothe the grass, which is today in the field, and to morrow is cast into the oven; *how much more* will he clothe you, O ye of little faith?" (Luke 12:28, emphasis added)

curiously gigantesque; it is full of camels leaping through needles and mountains hurled into the sea.[4] Morally it is equally terrific; he called himself a sword of slaughter, and told men to buy swords if they sold their coats for them.[5] That he used other even wilder words on the side of non-resistance greatly increases the mystery; but it also, if anything, rather increases the violence.

We cannot even explain it by calling such a being insane; for insanity is usually along one consistent channel. The maniac is generally a monomaniac. Here we must remember the difficult definition of Christianity already given; Christianity is a superhuman paradox whereby two opposite passions may blaze beside each other. The one explanation of the Gospel language that does explain it, is that it is the survey of one who from some supernatural height beholds some more startling synthesis.

"Christianity Belongs to the Dark Ages"

I take in order the next instance offered: the idea that Christianity belongs to the Dark Ages. Here I did not satisfy myself with reading modern generalisations; I read a little history. And in history I found that Christianity, so far from belonging to the Dark Ages, was the one path across the Dark Ages that was not dark. It was a shining bridge connecting two shining civilizations.

If any one says that the faith arose in ignorance and savagery the answer is simple: it didn't. It arose in the Mediterranean civilization in the full summer of the Roman Empire. The world was swarming with sceptics, and pantheism was as plain as the sun, when Constantine nailed the cross to the mast.[6] It is perfectly true that afterwards the ship sank; but it is far more extraordinary that

---

[4] Matt 19:24; Mark 11:23.

[5] Matt 10:34; Luke 22:36.

[6] Constantine I (272–337) was Roman emperor from AD 306 until his death, the first to convert to Christianity.

the ship came up again: repainted and glittering, with the cross still at the top.

This is the amazing thing the religion did: it turned a sunken ship into a submarine. The ark lived under the load of waters; after being buried under the debris of dynasties and clans, we arose and remembered Rome. If our faith had been a mere fad of the fading empire, fad would have followed fad in the twilight, and if the civilization ever reemerged (and many such have never reemerged) it would have been under some new barbaric flag. But the Christian Church was the last life of the old society and was also the first life of the new. She took the people who were forgetting how to make an arch and she taught them to invent the Gothic arch. In a word, the most absurd thing that could be said of the Church is the thing we have all heard said of it. How can we say that the Church wishes to bring us back into the Dark Ages? The Church was the only thing that ever brought us out of them.

The Irish Are Made Stagnant by Superstition

I added in this second trinity of objections an idle instance taken from those who feel such people as the Irish to be weakened or made stagnant by superstition. I only added it because this is a peculiar case of a statement of fact that turns out to be a statement of falsehood.

It is constantly said of the Irish that they are impractical. But if we refrain for a moment from looking at what is said about them and look at what is *done* about them, we shall see that the Irish are not only practical, but quite painfully successful. The poverty of their country, the minority of their members are simply the conditions under which they were asked to work; but no other group in the British Empire has done so much with such conditions. The Nationalists were the only minority that ever succeeded in twisting the whole British Parliament sharply out of its path. The Irish peasants are the only poor men in these islands who have forced their masters to disgorge. These people, whom we call priest-ridden, are the only Britons who will not be squire-ridden. And when I came to look at the actual Irish character, the case was the same. Irishmen are best at the specially *hard* professions—the trades of iron, the lawyer, and the soldier.

Turning Around the Objections

In all these cases, therefore, I came back to the same conclusion: the sceptic was quite right to go by the facts, only he had not looked at the facts. The sceptic is too credulous; he believes in newspapers or even in encyclopedias. Again the three questions left me with three very antagonistic questions. The average sceptic wanted to know how I explained the namby-pamby note in the Gospel, the connection of the creed with mediaeval darkness and the political impracticability of the Celtic Christians.

But I wanted to ask, and to ask with an earnestness amounting to urgency, "What is this incomparable energy which appears first in one walking the earth like a living judgment and this energy which can die with a dying civilization and yet force it to a resurrection from the dead; this energy which last of all can inflame a bankrupt peasantry with so fixed a faith in justice that they get what they ask, while others go empty away; so that the most helpless island of the Empire can actually help itself?"

There is an answer: it is an answer to say that the energy is truly from outside the world; that it is psychic, or at least one of the results of a real psychical disturbance. The highest gratitude and respect are due to the great human civilizations such as the old Egyptian or the existing Chinese. Nevertheless it is no injustice for them to say that only modern Europe has exhibited incessantly a power of self-renewal recurring often at the shortest intervals and descending to the smallest facts of building or costume. All other societies die finally and with dignity. We die daily. We are always being born again with almost indecent obstetrics.

It is hardly an exaggeration to say that there is in historic Christendom a sort of unnatural life: it could be explained as a supernatural life. It could be explained as an awful galvanic life working in what would have been a corpse. For our civilization *ought* to have died, by all parallels, by all sociological probability, in the Ragnorak of the end of Rome.[7] That is the weird inspiration of our estate: you and I have no business to be here at all. We are all *revenants*; all living Christians are dead pagans walking about. Just as Europe was about to be gathered in silence to Assyria and Babylon, something entered into its body. And Europe has had a strange life—it is not too much to say that it has had the *jumps*—ever since.

Summary

I have dealt at length with such typical triads of doubt in order to convey the main contention—that my own case for Christianity is rational; but it is not simple. It is an accumulation of varied facts, like the attitude of the ordinary agnostic.

But the ordinary agnostic has got his facts all wrong. He is a nonbeliever for a multitude of reasons; but they are untrue reasons. He doubts because the Middle Ages were barbaric, but they weren't; because Darwinism is demonstrated, but it isn't; because miracles do not happen, but they do; because monks were lazy, but they were very industrious; because nuns are unhappy, but they are particularly cheerful; because Christian art was sad and pale, but it was picked out in peculiarly bright colours and gay with gold; because modern science is moving away from the supernatural, but it isn't, it is moving towards the supernatural with the rapidity of a railway train.

---

[7] Ragnorak, in Norse mythology, refers to the great battle between the gods and the powers of evil, after which the world is submerged in water and resurfaces anew.

The Objection against Miracles

But among these million facts all flowing one way there is, of course, one question sufficiently solid and separate to be treated briefly, but by itself; I mean the objective occurrence of the supernatural.

In another chapter I have indicated the fallacy of the ordinary supposition that the world must be impersonal because it is orderly. A person is just as likely to desire an orderly thing as a disorderly thing. But my own positive conviction that personal creation is more conceivable than material fate, is, I admit, in a sense, undiscussable. I will not call it a faith or an intuition, for those words are mixed up with mere emotion, it is strictly an intellectual conviction; but it is a *primary* intellectual conviction like the certainty of self of the good of living.

Anyone who likes, therefore, may call my belief in God merely mystical; the phrase is not worth fighting about. But my belief that miracles have happened in human history is not a mystical belief at all; I believe in them upon human evidences as I do in the discovery of America. Upon this point there is a simple logical fact that only requires to be stated and cleared up.

Somehow or other an extraordinary idea has arisen that the disbelievers in miracles consider them coldly and fairly, while believers in miracles accept them only in connection with some dogma. The fact is quite the other way. The believers in miracles accept them (rightly or wrongly) because they have evidence for them. The disbelievers in miracles deny them (rightly or wrongly) because they have a doctrine against them.

Miracles and Democracy

The open, obvious, democratic thing is to believe an old apple-woman when she bears testimony to a miracle, just as you believe an old apple-woman when she bears testimony to a murder. The plain, popular course is to trust the peasant's word about the ghost exactly as far as you trust the peasant's word about the landlord. Being a peasant he will probably have a great deal of healthy agnosticism about both. Still you could fill the British Museum with evidence uttered by the peasant, and given in favour of the ghost.

If it comes to human testimony there is a choking cataract of human testimony in favour of the supernatural. If you reject it, you can only mean one of two things. You reject the peasant's story about the ghost either because the man is a peasant or because the story is a ghost story. That is, you either deny the main principle of democracy, or you affirm the main principle of materialism—the abstract impossibility of miracle. You have a perfect right to do so; but in that case you are the dogmatist. It is we Christians who accept all actual evidence—it is you rationalists who refuse actual evidence being constrained to do so by your creed. But I am not constrained by any creed in the matter, and looking impartially into certain miracles of mediaeval and modern times, I have come to the conclusion that they occurred.

Circular Arguments against Miracles

All argument against these plain facts is always argument in a circle. If I say, "Mediaeval documents attest certain miracles as much as they attest certain battles," they answer, "But mediaevals were superstitious"; if I want to know in what they were superstitious, the only ultimate answer is that they believed in the miracles. If I say "a peasant saw a ghost," I am told, "But peasants are so credulous." If I ask, "Why credulous?" the only answer is—that they see ghosts. Iceland is impossible because only stupid sailors have seen it; and the sailors are only stupid because they say they have seen Iceland.

It is only fair to add that there is another argument that the unbeliever may rationally use against miracles, though he himself generally forgets to use it. He may say that there has been in many miraculous stories a notion of spiritual preparation and acceptance: in short, that the miracle could only come to him who believed in it. It may be so, and if it is so how are we to test it? If we are inquiring whether certain results follow faith, it is useless to repeat wearily that (if they happen) they do follow faith. If faith is one of the conditions, those without faith have a most healthy right to laugh.

But they have no right to judge. Being a believer may be, if you like, as bad as being drunk; still if we were extracting psychological facts from drunkards, it would be absurd to be always taunting them with having been drunk. Suppose we were investigating whether angry men really saw a red mist before their eyes. Suppose sixty excellent householders swore that when angry they had seen this crimson cloud: surely it would be absurd to answer "Oh, but you admit you were angry at the time." They might reasonably rejoin (in a stentorian chorus), "How the blazes could we discover, without being angry, whether angry people see red?" So the saints and ascetics might rationally reply, "Suppose that the question is whether believers can see visions—even then, if you are interested in visions it is no point to object to believers." You are still arguing in a circle—in that old mad circle with which this book began.

The question of whether miracles ever occur is a question of common sense and of ordinary historical imagination: not of any final physical experiment. One may here surely dismiss that quite brainless piece of pedantry which talks about the need for "scientific conditions" in connection with alleged spiritual phenomena. If we are asking whether a dead soul can communicate with a living, it is ludicrous to insist that it shall be under conditions in which no two living souls in their senses would seriously communicate with each other. The fact that ghosts prefer darkness no more disproves the existence of ghosts than the fact that lovers prefer darkness disproves the existence of love. If you choose to say, "I will believe that Miss Brown called her fiance a periwinkle or, any other endearing term, if she will repeat the word before seventeen psychologists," then I shall reply, "Very well, if those are your conditions, you will never get the truth, for she certainly will not say it." It is just as unscientific as it is unphilosophical to be surprised that in an unsympathetic atmosphere certain extraordinary sympathies do not arise. It is as if I said that I could not tell if there was a fog because the air was not clear enough; or as if I insisted on perfect sunlight in order to see a solar eclipse.

Miracles and Common Sense

As a common-sense conclusion, such as those to which we come about sex or about midnight (well knowing that many details must in their own nature be concealed) I conclude that miracles do happen. I am forced to it by a conspiracy of facts: the fact that the men who encounter elves or angels are not the mystics and the morbid dreamers, but fishermen, farmers, and all men at once coarse and cautious; the fact that we all know men who testify to spiritualistic incidents but are not spiritualists, the fact that science itself admits such things more and more every day. Science will even admit the Ascension if you call it Levitation, and will very likely admit the Resurrection when it has thought of another word for it. I suggest the Regalvanisation.

But the strongest of all is the dilemma above mentioned, that these supernatural things are never denied except on the basis either of anti-democracy or of materialist dogmatism—I may say materialist mysticism. The sceptic always takes one of the two positions; either an ordinary man need not be believed, or an extraordinary event must not be believed. For I hope we may dismiss the argument against wonders attempted in the mere recapitulation of frauds, of swindling mediums or trick miracles. That is not an argument at all, good or bad. A false ghost disproves the reality of ghosts exactly as much as a forged banknote disproves the existence of the Bank of England—if anything, it proves its existence.

The Danger of "Mere Spirituality"

Given this conviction that the spiritual phenomena do occur (my evidence for which is complex but rational), we then collide with one of the worst mental evils of the age. The greatest disaster of the nineteenth century was this: that men began to use the word "spiritual" as the same as the word "good." They thought that to grow in refinement and uncorporeality was to grow in virtue.

When scientific evolution was announced, some feared that it would encourage mere animality. It did worse: it encouraged mere spirituality. It taught men to think that so long as they were passing from the ape they were going to the angel. But you can pass from the ape and go to the devil.

A man of genius, very typical of that time of bewilderment, expressed it perfectly. Benjamin Disraeli was right when he said he was on the side of the angels.[8] He was indeed; he was on the side of the fallen angels. He was not on the side of any mere appetite or animal brutality; but he was on the side of all the imperialism of the princes of the abyss; he was on the side of arrogance and mystery, and contempt of all obvious good.

Between this sunken pride and the towering humilities of heaven there are, one must suppose, spirits of shapes and sizes. Man, in encountering them, must make much the same mistakes that he makes in encountering any other varied types in any other distant continent. It must be hard at first to know who is supreme and who is subordinate. If a shade arose from the under world, and stared at Piccadilly, that shade would not quite understand the idea of an ordinary closed carriage. He would suppose that the coachman on the box was a triumphant conqueror, dragging behind him a kicking and imprisoned captive. So, if we see spiritual facts for the first time, we may mistake who is uppermost. It is not enough to find the gods; they are obvious; we must find God, the real chief of the gods. We must have a long historic experience in supernatural phenomena—in order to discover which are really natural.

In this light I find the history of Christianity, and even of its Hebrew origins, quite practical and clear. It does not trouble me

---

[8] In a debate on Darwin's *On the Origin of Species* in 1864, several years before his first term as prime minister of England, Benjamin Disraeli (1804–81) summarized the argument in this way: "The question is this—is man an ape or an angel? My lord, I am on the side of the angels."

to be told that the Hebrew god was one among many. I know he was, without any research to tell me so. Jehovah and Baal looked equally important, just as the sun and the moon looked the same size. It is only slowly that we learn that the sun is immeasurably our master, and the small moon only our satellite. Believing that there is a world of spirits, I shall walk in it as I do in the world of men, looking for the thing that I like and think good. Just as I should seek in a desert for clean water, or toil at the North Pole to make a comfortable fire, so I shall search the land of void and vision until I find something fresh like water, and comforting like fire; until I find some place in eternity, where I am literally at home. And there is only one such place to be found.

The Church as Living Teacher

I have now said enough to show (to any one to whom such an explanation is essential) that I have in the ordinary arena of apologetics, a ground of belief. In pure records of experiment (if these be taken democratically without contempt or favour) there is evidence first, that miracles happen, and second that the nobler miracles belong to our tradition. But I will not pretend that this curt discussion is my real reason for accepting Christianity instead of taking the moral good of Christianity as I should take it out of Confucianism.

I have another far more solid and central ground for submitting to it as a faith, instead of merely picking up hints from it as a scheme. And that is this: that the Christian Church in its practical relation to my soul is a living teacher, not a dead one. It not only certainly taught me yesterday, but will almost certainly teach me tomorrow. Once I saw suddenly the meaning of the shape of the cross; some day I may see suddenly the meaning of the shape of the mitre. One fine morning I saw why windows were pointed; some fine morning I may see why priests were shaven.

Plato has told you a truth; but Plato is dead. Shakespeare has startled you with an image; but Shakespeare will not startle you with any more. But imagine what it would be to live with such men still living, to know that Plato might break out with an original lecture tomorrow, or that at any moment Shakespeare might shatter everything with a single song. The man who lives in contact with what he believes to be a living Church is a man always expecting to meet Plato and Shakespeare tomorrow at breakfast. He is always expecting to see some truth that he has never seen before.

The Child in the Garden

There is one only other parallel to this position; and that is the parallel of the life in which we all began. When your father told you, walking about the garden, that bees stung or that roses smelt sweet, you did not talk of taking the best out of his philosophy. When the bees stung you, you did not call it an entertaining coincidence. When the rose smelt sweet you did not say "My father is a rude, barbaric symbol, enshrining (perhaps unconsciously) the deep delicate truths that flowers smell." No: you believed your father, because you had found him to be a living fountain of facts, a thing that really knew more than you; a thing that would tell you truth tomorrow, as well as today. And if this was true of your father, it was even truer of your mother; at least it was true of mine, to whom this book is dedicated.

Now, when society is in a rather futile fuss about the subjection of women, will no one say how much every man owes to the tyranny and privilege of women, to the fact that they alone rule education until education becomes futile: for a boy is only sent to be taught at school when it is too late to teach him anything. The real thing has been done already, and thank God it is nearly always done by women. Every man is womanised, merely by being born. They talk of the masculine woman; but every man is a feminised man. And if ever men walk to Westminster to protest against this female privilege, I shall not join their procession.

For I remember with certainty this fixed psychological fact; that the very time when I was most under a woman's authority, I was most full of flame and adventure. Exactly because when my mother said that ants bit they did bite, and because snow did come in winter (as she said); therefore the whole world was to me a fairyland of wonderful fulfilments, and it was like living in some Hebraic age, when prophecy after prophecy came true.

I went out as a child into the garden, and it was a terrible place to me, precisely because I had a clue to it: if I had held no clue it would not have been terrible, but tame. A mere unmeaning wilderness is not even impressive. But the garden of childhood was fascinating, exactly because everything had a fixed meaning which could be found out in its turn. Inch by inch I might discover what was the object of the ugly shape called a rake; or form some shadowy conjecture as to why my parents kept a cat.

So, since I have accepted Christendom as a mother and not merely as a chance example, I have found Europe and the world once more like the little garden where I stared at the symbolic shapes of cat and rake; I look at everything with the old elvish ignorance and expectancy. This or that rite or doctrine may look as ugly and extraordinary as a rake; but I have found by experience that such things end somehow in grass and flowers. A clergyman may be apparently as useless as a cat, but he is also as fascinating, for there must be some strange reason for his existence.

An Example: Virginity

I give one instance out of a hundred; I have not myself any instinctive kinship with that enthusiasm for physical virginity, which has certainly been a note of historic Christianity. But when I look not at myself but at the world, I perceive that this enthusiasm is not only a note of Christianity, but a note of Paganism, a note of high human nature in many spheres. The Greeks felt virginity when they carved Artemis, the Romans when they robed the vestals, the worst and wildest of the great Elizabethan playwrights clung to the literal purity of a woman as to the central pillar of the world. Above all, the modern world (even while mocking sexual innocence) has flung itself into a generous idolatry of sexual innocence—the great modern worship of children. For any man who loves children will agree that their peculiar beauty is hurt by a hint of physical sex. With all this human experience, allied with the Christian authority, I simply conclude that I am wrong, and the church right; or rather that I am defective, while the church is universal. It takes all sorts to make a church; she does not ask me to be celibate. But the fact that I have no appreciation of the celibates, I accept like the fact that I have no ear for music. The best human experience is against me, as it is on the subject of Bach. Celibacy is one flower in my father's garden, of which I have not been told the sweet or terrible name. But I may be told it any day.

Christianity as a Truth-Telling Thing

This, therefore, is, in conclusion, my reason for accepting the religion and not merely the scattered and secular truths out of the religion. I do it because the thing has not merely told this truth or that truth, but has revealed itself as a truth-telling thing. All other philosophies say the things that plainly seem to be true; only this philosophy has again and again said the thing that does not seem to be true, but is true. Alone of all creeds it is convincing where it is not attractive; it turns out to be right, like my father in the garden.

Theosophists for instance will preach an obviously attractive idea like re-incarnation; but if we wait for its logical results, they are spiritual superciliousness and the cruelty of caste. For if a man is a beggar by his own prenatal sins, people will tend to despise the beggar. But Christianity preaches an obviously unattractive idea, such as original sin; but when we wait for its results, they are pathos and brotherhood, and a thunder of laughter and pity; for only with original sin we can at once pity the beggar and distrust the king.

Men of science offer us health, an obvious benefit; it is only afterwards that we discover that by health, they mean bodily slavery and spiritual tedium. Orthodoxy makes us jump by the sudden brink of hell; it is only afterwards that we realise that jumping was an athletic exercise highly beneficial to our health. It is only afterwards that we realise that this danger is the root of all drama and romance.

The strongest argument for the divine grace is simply its ungraciousness. The unpopular parts of Christianity turn out when examined to be the very props of the people.

Adventure in the Land of Authority

The outer ring of Christianity is a rigid guard of ethical abnegations and professional priests; but inside that inhuman guard you will find the old human life dancing like children, and drinking wine like men; for Christianity is the only frame for pagan freedom. But in the modern philosophy the case is opposite; it is its outer ring that is obviously artistic and emancipated; its despair is within.

And its despair is this, that it does not really believe that there is any meaning in the universe; therefore it cannot hope to find any romance; its romances will have no plots. A man cannot expect any adventures in the land of anarchy. But a man can expect any number of adventures if he goes travelling in the land of authority. One can find no meanings in a jungle of scepticism; but the man will find more and more meanings who walks through a forest of doctrine and design. Here everything has a story tied to its tail, like the tools or pictures in my father's house; for it is my father's house. I end where I began—at the right end. I have entered at last the gate of all good philosophy. I have come into my second childhood.

The Primary Paradox of Christianity

But this larger and more adventurous Christian universe has one final mark difficult to express; yet as a conclusion of the whole matter I will attempt to express it. All the real argument about religion turns on the question of whether a man who was born upside down can tell when he comes right way up. The primary paradox of Christianity is that the ordinary condition of man is not his sane or sensible condition; that the normal itself is an abnormality. That is the inmost philosophy of the Fall.

In Sir Oliver Lodge's interesting new Catechism,[9] the first two questions were: "What are you?" and "What, then, is the meaning of the Fall of Man?" I remember amusing myself by writing my own answers to the questions; but I soon found that they were very broken and agnostic answers. To the question, "What are you?" I could only answer, "God knows." And to the question, "What is meant by the Fall?" I could answer with complete sincerity, "That whatever I am, I am not myself."

This is the prime paradox of our religion; something that we have never in any full sense known, is not only better than ourselves, but even more natural to us than ourselves. And there is really no test of this except the merely experimental one with which these pages began, the test of the padded cell and the open door. It is only since I have known orthodoxy that I have known mental emancipation. But, in conclusion, it has one special application to the ultimate idea of joy.

Joy: The Gigantic Secret of Christianity

It is said that Paganism is a religion of joy and Christianity of sorrow; it would be just as easy to prove that Paganism is pure sorrow and Christianity pure joy. Such conflicts mean nothing and lead nowhere. Everything human must have in it both joy and sorrow; the only matter of interest is the manner in which the two things are balanced or divided. And the really interesting thing is this, that the pagan was (in the main) happier and happier as he approached the earth, but sadder and sadder as he approached the heavens.

---

[9] Sir Oliver Lodge (1851–1940) was a British physicist and writer who tried to reconcile religion and science. Chesterton is referring to *The Substance of Faith Allied with Science: A Catechism for Parents and Teachers,* published in 1907.

The gaiety of the best Paganism, as in the playfulness of Catullus or Theocritus,[10] is, indeed, an eternal gaiety never to be forgotten by a grateful humanity. But it is all a gaiety about the facts of life, not about its origin. To the pagan the small things are as sweet as the small brooks breaking out of the mountain; but the broad things are as bitter as the sea. When the pagan looks at the very core of the cosmos he is struck cold. Behind the gods, who are merely despotic, sit the fates, who are deadly. Nay, the fates are worse than deadly; they are dead. And when rationalists say that the ancient world was more enlightened than the Christian, from their point of view they are right. For when they say "enlightened" they mean darkened with incurable despair.

It is profoundly true that the ancient world was more modern than the Christian. The common bond is in the fact that ancients and moderns have both been miserable about existence, about everything, while mediaevals were happy about that at least. I freely grant that the pagans, like the moderns, were only miserable about everything—they were quite jolly about everything else. I concede that the Christians of the Middle Ages were only at peace about everything—they were at war about everything else. But if the question turn on the primary pivot of the cosmos, then there was more cosmic contentment in the narrow and bloody streets of Florence than in the theatre of Athens or the open garden of Epicurus.[11] Giotto lived in a gloomier town than Euripides,[12] but he lived in a gayer universe.

The mass of men have been forced to be gay about the little things, but sad about the big ones. Nevertheless (I offer my last dogma defiantly) it is not native to man to be so. Man is more

---

[10] Gaius Valerius Catullus (84–54 BC) was a Latin poet of the late Roman Republic. Theocritus (300–260 BC) was a Sicilian poet.

[11] Epicurus (341–270 BC) was an ancient Greek philosopher and sage, and the founder of Epicureanism, a form of hedonism.

[12] Giotto di Bondone (1267–1337) was an Italian painter and architect from Florence. Euripides (480–406 BC) was a playwright of classical Athens.

himself, man is more manlike, when joy is the fundamental thing in him, and grief the superficial. Melancholy should be an innocent interlude, a tender and fugitive frame of mind; praise should be the permanent pulsation of the soul. Pessimism is at best an emotional half-holiday; joy is the uproarious labour by which all things live.

Yet, according to the apparent estate of man as seen by the pagan or the agnostic, this primary need of human nature can never be fulfilled. Joy ought to be expansive; but for the agnostic it must be contracted, it must cling to one corner of the world. Grief ought to be a concentration; but for the agnostic its desolation is spread through an unthinkable eternity.

This is what I call being born upside down. The sceptic may truly be said to be topsy-turvy; for his feet are dancing upwards in idle ecstasies, while his brain is in the abyss. To the modern man the heavens are actually below the earth. The explanation is simple; he is standing on his head; which is a very weak pedestal to stand on. But when he has found his feet again he knows it.

Christianity satisfies suddenly and perfectly man's ancestral instinct for being the right way up; satisfies it supremely in this; that by its creed joy becomes something gigantic and sadness something special and small. The vault above us is not deaf because the universe is an idiot; the silence is not the heartless silence of an endless and aimless world. Rather the silence around us is a small and pitiful stillness like the prompt stillness in a sickroom. We are perhaps permitted tragedy as a sort of merciful comedy: because the frantic energy of divine things would knock us down like a drunken farce. We can take our own tears more lightly than we could take the tremendous levities of the angels. So we sit perhaps in a starry chamber of silence, while the laughter of the heavens is too loud for us to hear.

Joy, which was the small publicity of the pagan, is the gigantic secret of the Christian.

And as I close this chaotic volume I open again the strange small book from which all Christianity came; and I am again haunted by a kind of confirmation. The tremendous figure which fills the Gospels towers in this respect, as in every other, above all the thinkers who ever thought themselves tall. His pathos was natural, almost casual. The Stoics, ancient and modern, were proud of concealing their tears. He never concealed His tears; He showed them plainly on His open face at any daily sight, such as the far sight of His native city. Yet He concealed something. Solemn supermen and imperial diplomatists are proud of restraining their anger. He never restrained His anger. He flung furniture down the front steps of the Temple, and asked men how they expected to escape the damnation of Hell. Yet He restrained something. I say it with reverence; there was in that shattering personality a thread that must be called shyness. There was something that He hid from all men when He went up a mountain to pray. There was something that He covered constantly by abrupt silence or impetuous isolation. There was some one thing that was too great for God to show us when He walked upon our earth; and I have sometimes fancied that it was His mirth.

Chapter Summary

In the final chapter, Chesterton opened with an important question that can be summed up this way: *Why not take the best effects of Christianity but leave behind the old, irrelevant doctrines?* Before answering, Chesterton considered a number of objections to Christianity—six criticisms bundled together in two triads (three objections each). In each case he considered the objection, pointed out the flawed facts or mistaken premises, then turned the objections around to become more evidence in favor of orthodoxy. He followed up these six objections with a lengthier reflection on a major objection in his day: the revolt against the reality of miracles and the existence of supernatural occurrences. His response pointed out the circular arguments deployed by those who disbelieve human testimony about miracles.

Finally, Chesterton returned to the question that opened the chapter. Can we not take what is good from Christianity but leave aside the distasteful doctrines? His response was to demonstrate the evidence for seeing Christianity as a "truth-telling thing." The church is a *living* teacher, and the authority of Christianity is what makes possible the freedom and joy we take for granted, as well as the adventurous romance of life we so desire. He concluded the book with a reflection on joy as the "gigantic secret of the Christian" and wondering out loud about the joy of God himself.

Discussion Questions

1. What are some of the most common objections to Christianity today, and how would Chesterton's approach and method respond to them?
2. How would you respond to someone who believes we should keep the best parts of Christianity but not feel obliged to accept the authority of the whole?

3. How is the Jesus of the Gospels surprising and different from the way he is often imagined by people unfamiliar with the Bible?
4. What does Chesterton mean by saying joy is what is most "fundamental" to humanity and the "gigantic secret of the Christian"?